JUNGLE MYTHS

Dec. 2002

To Carol & Paul,

From your fellow travelers for Jesus.

Keith & Marilyn

THE STORY OF ABWE'S MEDICAL WORK

ON THE AMAZON

JUNGLE MYTHS

Keith Kaynor

Association of Baptists for World Evangelism
P.O. Box 8585
Harrisburg, PA 17105-8585
(717) 774-7000

ABWE Canada
160 Adelaide St. South, Suite 205
London, Ontario N5Z 3L1
CANADA
(519) 690-1009

 PUBLISHING®

Unless otherwise noted, all scriptural quotations are taken from the King James Version of the Bible.

JUNGLE MYTHS

Harrisburg, Pennsylvania 17105

Library of Congress cataloging-in-publication data
(Application Pending)

Kaynor, Keith, 1944–
Jungle Myths: The Story of ABWE's Medical Work on the Amazon
Missions—Upper Amazon—Medicine—Non-Fiction
ISBN 1-888796-16-2 (Trade Paper)

Printed in the United States of America.

Table of Contents

Acknowledgements

To the following major contributors to this publication:

— My wife, Marilyn, for allowing me time away from home to visit the Amazon and time to write, and for her support and encouragement.

— Dr. Jack Sorg and Tom Peace for providing travel funds, and giving helpful travel assistance into and out of Brazil.

— Jennifer Sorg for interpreting, conducting interviews, and transcribing those interviews into English.

— Philip & Gecila Peace for taking me to various villages along the Amazon, interpreting and conducting interviews.

— Al & Kim Yoder for providing air transport, and for the gracious hospitality of the Yoder home and the fun of family night with the Yoder children.

— ABWE Publishing and editors Jeannie Lockerbie Stephenson and Kristen Stagg who provided the professional touch to complete this project.

— The missionaries and their supporters, who have worked and given to see the medical work along the Amazon develop and prosper to the glory of God.

I am grateful,
Keith Kaynor
April 1999

Foreword

Many people live with the myth of happy natives, living joyfully in harmony with nature, unencumbered by modern living. Developers, business people, and especially missionaries are accused of destroying the culture of native peoples. We read news reports or watch television programs showing lush forests stripped, thousands of trees burned and wasted, local people succumbing to Western diseases. "Just leave them alone" is the rallying cry of anthropologists.

This book has been written to expose 15 myths, replacing them with facts learned by missionaries of the Association of Baptists for World Evangelism (ABWE) over many years of living among—and loving—the people who live along the Amazon River.

Prologue

IN THE BEGINNING

by Paul Schlener

The Amazon jungle is possibly the most forbidding piece of land on the face of the Earth. Certainly it is the greatest expanse of boundless vegetation. From an airplane, passengers are convinced that the Amazon Basin must have been an ocean bottom at one time. Geologists agree. It is rainy, moldy and muddy, hot and humid, with no respite.

Nothing seems to dry completely. Continual rain makes for gigantic plants, serpentine rivers, endless swamps, and countless lakes. All of these, in conjunction with the equatorial sun, create the perfect environment to multiply plant and animal life, and to breed reptiles and insects, both visible and microscopic. Geography books call the Amazon Basin the "Green Hell."

Even in this modern era, it isn't easy for human beings to stay alive in this vast area and enjoy good health and a margin of comfort. Few technical advancements and little rationally ordered culture exists along the river in Brazil between Manaus, the capital city of the state of Amazonas, and the frontier where Brazil, Peru, and Colombia touch. This 1000-mile stretch of river was once the greatest unevangelized area in the world. ABWE refers to this area as the Central Amazon region.

Pioneer Missionaries

In 1943 Orville and Helen Floden were appointed to serve with ABWE. They arrived in 1944 in the town of Leticia, Colombia, where it touches the great Amazon River at the juncture of Peru, Colombia, and Brazil. The Flodens were a living example of what it means to be "saved to serve." They were multi-gifted, patient, long suffering, hard workers. Orville had been a truck driver for a beer distributor in Waterloo, Iowa. He later became a draftsman for the John Deere company. As a teenager Orville did acrobatics and was a great tap dancer. He and his girlfriend, Helen, became Christians and applied to Moody Bible Institute.

Helen was tireless. No one can remember her complaining about the things she had to do without. Young and old alike sought her counsel. Even her voice was soothing to those in trouble. She was concerned for the sick, and visited the suffering at all hours of day and night.

Two years after the Flodens' arrival in Leticia, Blake and Mary Rogers joined the Flodens. The Rogerses were a happy family. Jeannie was a little girl and Ruthie was on the way when they climbed out of the Catalina flying boat. Although Mary was reserved, she was a good teacher and organist, greatly enhancing the church work. Blake was husky and athletic, "the Good Humor Man" of the crowd. Joviality was one of his strong points and he was a great preacher wherever he ministered.

These two families were well prepared for pioneer work. They were dedicated servants and quickly became fluent in the language. Together they kept their shoulders to the wheel to establish the local church and do river evangelism.

In 1950 Jack and Joyce Looney, with their two little boys, Roy and Terry, arrived in the town of Benjamin Constant, 12 miles around river bends from Leticia, where the Javari River contributes its generous volume to the mighty Amazon and serves as the border between Brazil and Peru. Benjamin Constant, on the Brazilian side of the frontier, was another gateway into the endless unevangelized Central Amazon region. Twelve miles wasn't far to live from the Flodens and Rogerses, but there was no communication and the only mode of travel was by water. The pioneer-spirited Looneys qualified superbly for this work. The Texan couple was the last word in Southern hospitality. Jack and Joyce evangelized in Benjamin Constant and planted a church there. Later Jack constructed a 30-foot boat and did river evangelism as far up as he could navigate the tributaries of the Javari River on both the Brazilian and Peruvian sides of the narrow streams.

The Schlener Brothers

But the thousand-mile stretch of unevangelized Central Amazon territory still hadn't been touched with the gospel. In August of 1951, ABWE sent the two Schlener brothers, John and Paul, and their families to the Central Amazon region to join the Flodens, Rogerses, and Looneys. The tiny Central Amazon field council assigned the Schleners to spearhead evangelism into the first 100 miles of that forbidding area.

Both Schlener brothers graduated from BIOLA, John in 1949 and Paul in 1950. But to say that the Schlener brothers were prepared to meet the challenges that faced them in the Amazon would be the overstatement of the century. Both were WWII vets. John, a bombardier/navigator on a B-17 bomber, was wounded on his thirteenth mission over Germany. He knew how to strap on a parachute, find places on the map, look through a bomb sight, and punch the button.

Paul served on a baby flattop in the South Pacific. He became an expert paint chipper, a proficient swab jockey, learned to tie a half-dozen different kinds of knots, and to shove 40mm shells up to the first loader.

After the Schleners made survey trips into the area, they were able to purchase 90 acres of virgin jungle bordering the village of Santa Rita. To make the purchase official, the property had to have a name. The Schleners called it The Port of Two Brothers. Enough jungle was cleared to make a temporary dwelling, until lumber became available from a military sawmill some 120 miles upriver from the Port of Two Brothers.

Life in the jungle was a vast contrast to life in the United States. When they arrived on the Amazon each family had two children, the youngest was Paul and Jessie's Leanne, only four months old. In those days, no Pampers® were available, no electricity, and no plumbing for bathrooms or kitchens. Outhouses and bucket brigades did the trick until they could catch rainwater from the roof. A hotline to their heavenly Father was the only communication. Pokey river boats went by, sometimes six weeks apart, with a skimpy supply of stuff to purchase. A dugout canoe with a five-horsepower outboard could travel to Benjamin Constant in 18 hours—if gasoline was available and if the weather wasn't too bad. If a doctor happened to be in Benjamin Constant, it was good fortune to find him sober.

Some 700 Christians in the United States had promised to pray regularly for the Schlener families as they struggled to reach people with the gospel. God protected and blessed the two families in countless and wonderful ways.

John and Paul enjoyed the challenges of the forbidding Amazon jungle. Their wives, Fran and Jessie, petite ladies, were great examples of rugged perseverance against everything that opposed their efforts to maintain a comfortable family life. They weren't fearless. They wondered at times how they could make it. But they never backed down as they made do with what they had, often under disagreeable circumstances.

Building a Home in the Jungle

Finally, lumber was ready for the construction of the Schleners' permanent homes. The beautiful red mahogany boards and beams were bunched together at the Colombian sawmill and tied securely with vines into two, 20-ton rafts. Orville and Helen floated the first raft the 120 miles downriver to the Port of Two Brothers during high-water season when the river's current is faster than normal. Nearly a year later, John and Paul left their families behind to float the second raft down from Colombia during the dry season when sandbars were a hazard. The trip took three days and nights. Lack of know-how and power tools made the construction of the 1,400-square-foot houses extremely slow.

No programs for language study existed at the time, so the hard work of becoming fluent in the language was a catch-as-catch-can process. Shortly before boarding the plane in Philadelphia, the families were presented with two language study books. The donor remarked, "The Lord bless you as you study the language."

Medical Beginnings

John and Paul were forced to do what they could to help sick people. Ax and machete gashes, pinkeye, malaria, amoebic dysentery, tuberculosis, intestinal parasites, sores that wouldn't heal, combined with myriad maladies that couldn't be diagnosed by untrained pioneers, kept the men busy and anxious. Tooth decay with gingivitis was a sad situation, especially among mothers who had no prenatal care. The extraction of nearly 10,000 teeth helped some people, but that was like trying to bail out a lake with a bucket.

Poisonous snake bites were disastrous and took many lives. The victims were taken first to witch doctors for treatment. When the witch doctors gave up and the victims were near death, they were brought to John and Paul. After a few years the missionaries gained the confidence of most, and people started to bring the victims, writhing in pain, soon after they had been bitten.

From the Port of Two Brothers, river evangelization was done, and primary schools were started for both Brazilians and Ticuna Indians. The Brazilian school continued for 19 years. Indians who studied in the schools at the Port of Two Brothers started nine of their own private schools in their respective villages.

After filming one of the drunken orgies during a festivity celebrating puberty rites in 1953, prayer interest increased phenomenally among the Schleners' supporting constituency, and God's blessing came down in a mighty way among the Ticunas.

Little did the Schleners realize when they purchased The Port of Two Brothers that they were positioned in the geographic center of the Ticuna Indian population. The first Indian congregation had an attendance of between 600 and 1,000 depending on the stage of the river, the main highway to church. In 1991 when Paul, the last of the Schlener brothers, left Amazonas, 13 organized local churches were functioning under the leadership of lay pastors.

MYTH NO. 1

Everyone Trusts Us

"I don't have any money. Why are they so nice to me?"

With difficulty, Dona Dulce pulled herself upright on the hospital bed, leaned forward, and picked up the powder-blue bathrobe at the foot of the bed. Several times she ran her leathery hands over the soft, luxurious material. As she pulled it on, the robe enfolded her like a pleasant hug. She smiled. Never had she owned anything like this before. What a wonderful gift!

Frightened, but with no other place to go, Dona Dulce had arrived at the Amazonas Baptist Hospital at Santo Antônio do Içá several weeks earlier. Only 40 years of age, she could have passed for 60. Six months before, she had delivered a stillborn baby and had been ill ever since. Her wrinkled skin and round, puffy face indicated kidney problems. Lab tests and X-rays confirmed a severe kidney infection and congestive heart failure.

"It was days before Dona Dulce worked up the courage to talk with us," said ABWE missionary lab and X-ray technician Sue Thomson. One day, while having a chest X-ray taken, Dona Dulce whispered to Sue, "Do you have a dress for me?" Patients often asked this question, so Sue promised Dona Dulce she would see if anything was available. Later, Sue asked Rocilda, a Brazilian nurse, about Dona Dulce's situation.

The old-looking 40-year-old woman was from a small village an hour (by speedboat) from Santo Antônio. Because she had been sick for so long, Dona Dulce's family threw her and her clothes out of the house and sent her to the hospital.

Sue Thomson continued, "I walked home, found a bathrobe, blouse, skirt, and some underwear and took them to her. Dona Dulce accepted them without a word."

Rocilda noticed Dona Dulce's new clothes and her proud smile. But she also noticed her fear. The suspicious patient asked herself, *Why are these people so nice to me? I don't have any money; how will I pay for the meals I'm eating? Look at all the medicines I'm taking. How can I pay for them? And this robe—how can I pay Dona Susana* (Sue Thomson) *for it and the other clothes?*

Days passed before Dona Dulce had the courage to voice her fears and, when she did, it was not to an American, but to another Brazilian. "You don't have to pay for anything. We don't charge our patients," Rocilda told her.

"But why?" Dona Dulce couldn't believe such services were free. "Why would anyone care about me? Look how ugly I am—all wrinkled and old. I'm not good for anything!"

What happened next is what energizes missionary nurses, doctors, and church planters: Dona Dulce was about to hand the missionaries their ultimate spiritual paycheck.

"It's because we love God and you. He loves you, too. We want to show you His love and care," Rocilda gently explained. It was the right time to tell the rejected "old" woman about the Lord Jesus Christ and how He died on the cross for her.

Dona Dulce frowned. "I've heard that missionaries give things to people, but after people believe in this Jesus, they are fattened up and sent to America to become canned meat."

"No, that's not true," Rocilda assured her. "My family has been here since the first missionary family arrived, and no Brazilian Christian has ever disappeared." Though she remained guarded and unresponsive, Dona Dulce began to relax.

A few days later, Maria, another nurse, experienced abdominal pain and was placed in the bed next to Dona Dulce. Maria spent her recovery time crocheting.

When Sue noticed Dona Dulce watching the crocheting with interest, she located a crochet hook and yarn. Handing them to Maria, Sue suggested, "Could you show God's love to Dona Dulce by teaching her to crochet?"

Later, the budding student called Sue over to show her a bright orange square. Pleased with herself, Dona Dulce announced, "It's to put a hot pan on."

That night, a third nurse told the sick woman about the love of Jesus, and Dona Dulce believed in Jesus Christ as her Savior.

One week later, Dona Dulce's tired heart gave out, her spirit left the worn body and went to heaven.

North Americans might imagine everyone in a developing area automatically trusts a modern American hospital, especially one whose staff is motivated by God's love. But that's a myth, as Dona Dulce's story shows.

While most Brazilians *do* trust the hospital, some don't. Over the years, the Amazonas Baptist Hospital has established itself for hundreds of miles up and down the Amazon River as a high quality, compassionate expression of the living God.

This book tells the story of the Amazonas Baptist Hospital, located about 1,750 miles upriver from the Atlantic Ocean in the Brazilian Amazon. The hospital was built by the Association of Baptists for World Evangelism (ABWE), headquartered in Harrisburg, Pennsylvania.

Let's visit the hospital. Starting in the United States, we fly south out of Miami, Florida, over northwestern South America, before encountering the Amazon River, which Jere Van Dyke, writing in National Geographic *calls a "liquid highway that defines life in this region." From the air we see miles of what looks like giant broccoli stretching from the river to the horizon. It is this lush vegetation that stirs up fervor on the part of the environmentalists. What are the facts about the rain forests of the Amazon Basin?*

MYTH NO. 2

The Rain Forests Are Gone

"The jungle is disappearing because of road builders, loggers— and missionaries."

Posted in the motel lobby in Leticia, Colombia, was an article by Adam Hochscheld titled "Back to Nature: Amazon Indians Return to the Rain Forests." The article read:

> Few places on earth have had their indigenous cultures more shattered than the Amazon. The jungle is eroding before road builders, loggers, cattle ranchers and slash-and-burn farmers. Their numbers drastically shrunken, the remaining Amazon Indians are migrating to towns and cities in search of work on the impoverished margins of the machine-based civilization that has largely destroyed their own.
>
> (*Examiner Magazine*, July 23, 1995)

The rain forests are *not* gone. It is true that satellite photos show clear-cut patches where trees once stood. But inflammatory articles in the North American press make it sound as if 60 to 80 percent of the trees are gone. Although such articles make great press, they are not true. In actual fact, approximately 10 percent of the Brazilian rain forest has been destroyed, the majority of it around large cities where much more than just trees are affected by pollution and the relentless drive toward industrialization. The articles carry some elements of truth, but contain several problems:

1. It seems the purpose of the articles is to inflame world opinion; conditions are exaggerated and the authors smugly criticize Brazil as though North America had no environmental sins of its own.
2. Industrialized nations—and those who battle over resources in global economic warfare—are eager to gobble up natural resources wherever they are found, so their environmentalist opponents are not totally out of place in screaming, "The lungs of the planet are gone."
3. Hard-core environmentalists who write inflammatory articles don't balance the needs of local people with the ideal of nature.
4. Some environmentalists hint that the motive of every white man in the area is exploitation, which is simply not true.
5. Others give the impression that missionaries are bothering the happy natives, but say nothing about the initiative taken by nationals to leave their villages and seek out the modern world.

Admitted Misuse of the Land

Some years ago, an American industrialist built a paper plant in the Brazilian rain forest in a unique way. He floated huge barges—the two halves of his factory—up the river to a lake he had created. Bulldozing the neck of the lake shut, and filling in the lake around the barges, he bolted the two halves of his paper factory together and set about cutting down huge tracts of land to feed his paper mill.

At this point, world opinion mobilized on the side of Brazilian vegetation and blasted Brazil for granting the permits which allowed exploitation of the rain forest. Straight-arming further criticism, Brazil reacted by withdrawing permits. In any case, the industrialist's billion-dollar project failed, and he sold his plant (at enormous financial loss) to a national consortium. Sections of land, five to ten miles square, had been logged off. In such cases, the jungle does not reforest for a long time. This was not good for the region. Protecting the rain forests became a cause for the American press, just as "Save the Whales" was in 1983.

The Amazon Basin—about half of South America—reaches into parts of six countries. Some parts have been exploited for centuries, while other areas remain untouched.

What Is the Situation?

In order to gain a balanced view of the situation, it is helpful to review some significant watersheds in Brazil's environmental history. Although some of this happened outside of Amazonas, the effects were felt nationwide. In Joseph A. Page's book *The Brazilians*, he tells of the industrial city of Cubatão, located just 13 miles from São Paulo and close to Santos, the largest port city in all of South America. It was created specifically to encourage both national and international development of business. Nations whose own anti-pollution laws rendered expensive equipment obsolete were permitted to set up factories—with the polluting machinery in place—in Brazil. Many such plants were located in Cubatão, routinely referred to by Brazilians and internationals alike as the "Valley of Death" or "the most polluted place on earth."

A 1980 investigation of this city, home to more than 100,000 people, revealed that daily industrial dumping equalled more than *2,500 tons* of poisonous waste into nearby streams, killing vegetation and causing severe deformities among the offspring of both animals and humans who consumed these deadly waters. Vegetation on the slopes of the plateau above the city ceased to exist. It was as if all of nature groaned under the toxins that spewed from smokestacks into the sky, and from drainage pipes into the waterways.

In 1984 a pipeline carrying diesel oil to the national gas company's refinery in Cubatão exploded, setting fire to the shantytowns where most of the city's inhabitants live. While official estimates set the death toll at 100, unofficial sources claim the number was six to eight times what police reported. But this tragic incident was treated as part of the price required for modernization.

The year 1988 again saw world attention focused on Amazonas when Chico Mendes, an internationally recognized leader of Brazilian rubber tappers seeking to protect Brazil's rain forests, was shot down by assassins in a town on the western edge of Amazonas. Not only was the plight of nature at stake, so were the lives of individuals opposing the businesses that could potentially provide jobs for Brazil's lower classes.

Mining, too, has wreaked havoc on the natural landscape in southeastern Brazil. Iron ore, gold, bauxite, and copper are just a few of the exports carved, literally, out of the ground. In addition to the gaping craters left at the mining locations, deadly mineral waste contaminated local rivers. Three thousand *tons* of mercury were released into the Amazon since the 1950's and three hundred tons into the Madeira River between 1979 and 1987 alone.

Environmentalists Decry the Cutting of the Rain Forest

Deforestation is much more difficult to estimate accurately, especially when jungle encompasses the 1.3 million square miles that comprise the Amazon Basin.

ABWE missionary pilot Al Yoder has flown the length of the Amazon. He reports, "I have not seen widespread deforestation." Granted, vision extends only a few miles on each side of the airplane at an altitutde of 5,000 feet, but the river makes many loops and a pilot can see several thousand square miles flying a straight line from one location to another.

It is difficult to argue against satellite photos, which show that nearly one-tenth of the dense jungle vegetation has disappeared. While most areas reforest with amazing speed, in some locations the poor soil content of the ground, below what was once a tree canopy, means that the area will remain without plant life for decades, possibly even longer.

To cut down the entire Brazilian rain forest, however, the small jungle population would need to stay on the job constantly to keep ahead of the heavy rainfall and naturally productive soil. It is difficult to burn down small patches of jungle. After vegetation is cut, it must dry for days before it will burn. A built-in, climate-controlled fire extinguisher is provided by 200 inches of annual rainfall.

ABWE missionary to the Amazon Beth Peace said this about deforestation:

"Who are we to tell the Brazilians that they cannot better their lives? My mom bought land in the state of Washington just after the road to Seattle went through. The whole area was standing timber. Mom put up an army surplus tent, where we lived for a long time. She and my dad, when he was sober, and we kids, used a big crosscut saw and dropped enough trees to build a little house. Over the years, other trees came down. Today, not an original tree stands on the place. You just try telling my mom she could not cut down those trees to better her family! The frontier settlers cut down trees to build homes, farms, and towns. Who do we Americans think we are to tell indigenous Brazilian people they can't better themselves?

"North America was founded to allow people to worship God, and to pursue a better life. It's hypocritical for us to tell others they can't do the same. The wealthy nations of the world have exploited their resources and polluted the air, and they want other nations to live off the crumbs that fall from their table. When North Americans are asked who it is they are trying to save the world for, they often answer that they are saving the world to make a better place for their children and grandchildren. To this, the poor in many nations would answer, 'If I don't feed my family now, there won't be any grandchildren!'"

Yes, there is some old-growth cutting. Yes, the satellite photos show encroachment of civilization. Yes, there are significant areas that have been burned off. But we North Americans, who turned the prairie grasslands into the breadbasket of the world and clear-cut vast areas of our own forests, and harvested pine in the early 1900's beyond what was healthy, should think twice before we criticize a developing nation. Are we going to pretend that there was no exploitation of the American West?

On the other hand, to blithely ignore a valid concern that contributes to global warming, and to treat carelessly the blatant disregard for a valuable natural resource is gross mismanagement of godly stewardship on the part of Christians.

Big companies—generally non-Brazilian—do cause damage. But local people also cause damage as they eke out a living. The complaint is made that Westerners—including missionaries—invade the primeval jungle, forcing the indigenous people to abandon their villages and move into towns and cities. The truth is that primitive people often leave the jungle, seeking civilization. There are adequate reasons for this movement.

- Indians want a market for their products. If the government builds roads, local people can get their produce to market in a timely manner.
- Native peoples want protection from drug lords.
- Like people everywhere, they look for a reasonable level of medical care.

Medical missions has long been known to introduce people to a God who loves and cares about the needs of those He created. The goal of ABWE medical missions is more specific: to be a witness for Jesus Christ, with the result that people believe and churches are established.

The Amazon is a harsh environment, with deadly insects and reptiles, significant diseases, and other physical dangers. Would anyone even consider sending a single woman to such hostile territory?

MYTH NO. 3

Single Women Can't Make It on the Amazon

"This is the frontier! No place for a woman."

The Amazon is a foreboding area where travel is uncertain. It's the frontier, a man's world. ABWE thought it was no place for a single woman. Tell that to Lois Wantoch, whose medical work on the Amazon preceded the hospital.

Lois was born in 1939, the second of four children. As a farm girl growing up in Nebraska, she didn't know what a missionary was. Yet farm life was excellent preparation for the Brazilian frontier.

On the farm she gathered the eggs, milked the cows, fed the dog, made her own clothes, and planted her share of the family garden. As a child, Lois saw her family improvise or do without. Honesty and discipline were woven into the values of her home.

Her family sat together in church every Sunday. The children were expected to listen and be alert, even if the messages were usually on an adult level.

Lois' mother read bedtime Bible stories to her almost every night. Describing her infant baptism, catechism classes, and religious training, however, Lois says, "It was a religion of works without salvation." Though the parochial school taught her to say the books of the Bible forward and backward, Lois was not a Christian.

While Lois was still a young child, God started working in her mother's life. Home with the children in pre-television days, Lois' mother began to hear the gospel on the radio. Learning spiritual truth over the radio that she didn't hear Sunday mornings at church, she was awakened to her need of salvation.

After her salvation experience, Lois' mother began to speak to her husband about salvation. She tried to interest him in visiting other churches which might preach the same things she had been hearing on the radio. Little by little, she convinced her husband to look around. A tolerant man, he went, though he did not have any special interest in any other religion.

When Lois was 11 years old, the family went to an evangelistic meeting in a neighboring town where Ray Cutchen was preaching. Her dad went forward, making a profession of faith in Jesus Christ. Two nights later, the evangelist was preaching on Isaiah 53, and the Holy Spirit was at work convicting Lois. Evangelist Cutchen preached that Jesus Christ was like a sheep going to be slaughtered, and that He gave His life for those who would believe. Lois gave her life to God, believing in Jesus Christ as her Savior.

Sampling several different churches, the family decided on the Christian and Missionary Alliance Church during Lois' high school years. She also got involved in the American Sunday School Union, through which she taught Vacation Bible School in rural schools.

At the Christian and Missionary Alliance Church, Lois had her first exposure to missions: stories, films, and missionary speakers. Lois thought, *Wouldn't it be great to live the adventurous life of a missionary? Going to all those exciting places!*

After high school, Lois attended Bible school for one year, then transferred into nurses' training. The nursing school had a "Big Sister Program" that linked upper classmen with first-year students. A friend who had been a fellow teacher through the American Sunday School Union was Lois' Big Sister. She attended Temple Baptist Church in Omaha and invited Lois to go with her.

At Temple Baptist, Lois heard more missionary speakers and realized missions was more than just adventure and travel. She saw that the real purpose in missions was to win the lost to Christ.

The Cook's Question

Two things were ending: nurses' training and Lois' interest in being a missionary. Past the naive stage about missions, Lois turned her attention to finding a good job. Having been raised with few extras, she looked forward to being able to buy what she wanted.

With cooled interest, Lois' view now was, "Lord, I see the need for missions. I want to get a good position in a hospital, marry, have a family and a nice home, and work my way up in the nursing profession. I will be glad to help others be missionaries, but please don't call me to the mission field."

After three years of nurses' training, Lois returned to Bible school for two years. As graduation approached, classmates announced their post-graduation plans: "I am going to the mission field;" "I am going teach in a Christian school;" "I am going to be a pastor's wife."

Lois was embarrassed because she didn't have specific direction from God. Years later, Lois said about this discomforting situation, "I was struggling because the Lord had a plan for me, but I had my own ideas. At that time, I didn't realize why I didn't know God's will for my life. Now I know why; I was resisting the Lord. I was not ready to accept what the Lord had for me, and He had to make me willing before He would show me what He wanted for my life."

Lois always enjoyed summer camp. When she was too old to be a camper, she returned as counselor, nurse, or cook. God used the head cook to speak to her. "Lois, have you ever considered missions?" Dismissing the question, Lois casually said, "Sure, I've considered missions." Though the cook didn't pursue the subject, the Lord did. God began to deal with Lois. The Lord wouldn't let her forget the cook's question. Time and again the question returned to her mind. She *had* to answer that question to the Lord. This weight would not lift.

Lois was coming to a crisis, a spiritual watershed. She said to herself, "Lord, I am convinced that You don't want me to be a missionary, but I am a logical person, so I'll make a balance sheet." On one side, she wrote down reasons why she would *not* be a good missionary, and on the other side, factors that would lead her to be a missionary.

Years after this scene, Lois described it as follows: "I quickly filled up the negative side with all my excuses. When you are looking for excuses, if you run short, Satan is right there to provide more than you might need."

Excuses, Excuses

- "Through high school, Bible school, and nurses' training, I never had the opportunity to study a foreign language. My high school stopped teaching Spanish before I entered high school and started teaching German after I graduated, so God does not want me on the mission field."
- "God, I've never been outside the continental United States. The world is foreboding to me. Legal matters! Travel! Lord, I've never even been on an airplane. How would I find my way around? How would I find a place to live?"
- "I can't go as a single person. If I were married and had a husband to take care of my concerns, it would be different. There are too many problems to which I don't see the answers. No, Lord, I can't be a missionary."

The Other Side of the Balance Sheet

The Lord led Lois to these verses of Scripture: "Faithful is He that calleth you, who also will do it" (1 Thessalonians 5:24); "Being confident of this very thing, that He which hath begun a good work in you will perform until the day of Jesus Christ" (Philippians 1:6.) Lois' side of the balance sheet said, "I can't do it." That was true, but the other side said, "God can do it."

God was not looking for someone who had a mastery of foreign languages, or lots of talent. He did not need a travel veteran, or a legal whiz. God was looking for someone who was available to Him, and dependent upon Him to show the way.

Having come to that spiritual vantage point, Lois had peace. The heaviness was lifted. "I didn't have the big question hanging over my head."

But she was still getting accustomed to the idea of being a missionary. Her attitude was, "Okay, Lord, I will take some steps. I'll write to a mission board, and even fill out an application. If at any time along the way You want to shut the door, that's all right with me."

Instead of closing the door, the Lord kept opening doors. Her application to the Association of Baptists for World Evangelism was accepted. While some prospective missionaries face candidate class with a fearful sense of being examined and scrutinized, Lois went with a spirit of adventure.

Years later, Lois reflected, "God has been faithful to those verses He pointed out to me when I was struggling to yield myself to Him. He has gone ahead of me, guided me, protected me, and given joy and satisfaction as I have served Him."

Declaring for the Amazon

After Lois was accepted to attend ABWE's candidate class in 1965, she thought, *Candidate class is going to be great, like a month at camp*. It never crossed her mind that the mission might turn her down.

During the month-long candidate class held at that time, missionary candidates were introduced to potential places of service: Argentina, Spain, Japan, and many others. Lois' medical interests prompted inquiries about medical evangelism. ABWE had three medical works at that time: hospitals in Bangladesh and the Philippines, and a small work on the Amazon in Brazil. A medical clinic in Peru also loomed on the horizon.

During her college days, Lois had seen the 35mm film *The Port of Two Brothers*, showing the work of John and Paul Schlener along the Amazon River. After watching the film, Lois asked John, "Could you use nurses on the Amazon?" "Yes," he replied, "but we are not accepting single women for the Amazon." Characteristically, John offered a solution to that problem: "Get yourself a husband and come on down."

Seeing the film sparked Lois' interest in the Amazon. The Amazon was rural, just like her Nebraska roots. As she talked with various people during candidate class, she felt that God was giving her a special interest in South America in general, and in the Amazon in particular.

Single

But what about John Schlener's statement that the mission was not accepting single women missionaries for the Amazon? Would ABWE refuse her? The Amazon field council was consulted, and word came back that they would not accept one woman by herself, but if two single women would come as a team, they would be accepted. At the time, Lois was the only one in the class interested in the Amazon. By the end of the classes, however, another single woman, Nancy Crosser, a teacher of missionary children, was interested in the Amazon. So Nancy and Lois were appointed as a team to the Amazon.

Deputation

The process of visiting churches to raise up a support team was unfamiliar territory. Lois was comfortable with telling an illustrated Bible story to eight or ten children, but speaking in front of a church was another matter. She thought, *All those adults! I will be behind the pulpit with my knees shaking. I can't do this. But if I don't do it, I'll never get to the mission field.*

Instructed to arrive at churches early, Lois did. Sometimes even

30 minutes before the pastor arrived. Hers was the only car in the parking lot. Sometimes, fear seized her: *No one knows I'm here. I could turn around and leave, and no one would know I'd been here.*

Lois consulted missionaries for current information, and told the churches what was happening. Sometimes after she spoke, people asked her, "How many years have you been on the field?" She replied, "I have not been there yet." Because of her enthusiasm, people thought she had already been there.

Lois relates, "I had butterflies in my stomach as I was being introduced. But then a wonderful thing happened. Once I started talking about the Amazon, I was comfortable speaking in the churches. What I thought would be an impossible task, the Lord turned into an adventure. God turned my nervousness into enthusiasm."

Out of the Deputation Nest

After two years of traveling from California to Maryland and from Canada to the Mexican border, Lois was not sure she wanted it to end; not sure about the big step of leaving for the field. "I can easily get in a rut. To do something new, sometimes I need a push."

Whereas deputation had become a comfortable nest, learning a new language loomed large and daunting.

Her arrival at the language school was disappointing. She met a couple in Miami who were to accompany her to Fortaleza, Brazil. She had telegrammed ahead to the missionaries in Fortaleza about her arrival. When the plane landed, her traveling companions were hugged and warmly welcomed, but no one was there to meet Lois. *Lord, did You bring me here so I'd be ignored?* The telegram had been distorted and no one expected her to arrive at that time.

As a result of her support coming in quickly, Lois' co-worker Nancy Crosser arrived for language study one year before Lois. Because Lois knew no Portuguese, she was convinced her co-worker knew everything, and she felt intimidated.

Three Spiritual Hurdles

Nancy taught in a school for missionary children in Fortaleza while Lois did her language study. During that year, Nancy began to doubt. Brazil? Yes. Amazon? Not sure. Nancy reached a point that she no longer had peace about going to the Amazon.

Then a romantic interest developed, further distracting her. When Nancy withdrew from the Amazon field, Lois was left with no partner—a condition for acceptance imposed by the Central Amazon field council.

It was difficult for Nancy to tell Lois about her lack of peace regarding the Amazon, but Lois said, "Don't worry about this, Nancy. If the Lord wants me on the Amazon, He will have a way to get me there. I wouldn't want you to go just for my sake. God will get me there with you or without you."

Having been brave and full of faith as she spoke to Nancy, Lois now had to address the Central Amazon field council. Would they accept her on her own? She wrote a letter to the field council, communicating her call from God to the Amazon, and entrusting the decision to them.

Besides losing her co-worker, a second spiritual barrier for Lois came from Brazilian Christians who questioned the wisdom of her destination. They said, "The Amazon? Are you sure it's safe up there? That's the frontier; hardly a part of civilized Brazil. Isn't that where you have to wear boots up to your hips and use mosquito nets all the time to ward off the insects from the swamps?" Her response was, "That's where God has called me, and that's where I have peace about going."

Lois did not find out about the third spiritual hurdle until later: the attitudes of fellow missionaries. Years after Lois became a vital member of the ABWE Central Amazon missionary team, she learned that the missionaries had held a lengthy discussion about whether or not to accept her. Would she be a burden to the other missionaries? Would she frequently ask for help to do repairs around the house? Would there be moral problems with nationals?

Finally, one of the married women, Dot Blakslee, said, "If the Lord has called her to the Amazon, who are we to say 'NO'?" A vote was taken and Lois has been on the Amazon ever since.

Though unaware of the debate her presence stirred, the rookie was made to understand that she would have to paddle her own canoe.

Bunking with the Kids

Getting started in any new endeavor is stressful. Orientation humbles us all. One of the toughest things for Lois was staying in the homes of various missionaries, where she normally roomed with the kids. Many homes on the mission field do not have guest rooms. While her fellow missionaries were kind and generous, still, they had to move over for her, which created tension.

Desperate for privacy to pray or cry aloud, weary of using someone else's typewriter and imposing on their space, Lois needed her own place. Month after month of living out of a suitcase was grinding her down.

What got her through the tears, the struggles, and the language study was the certainty that God wanted her there. That sustained her. The climate wasn't a big problem; Nebraska can be hot, too. Nor was food adjustment a big hurdle; she had been taught to eat whatever was set before her.

When she got discouraged, Lois would go for a walk and talk to Brazilians. Soon her mind would be off her problems as she got involved in other people's lives. She made numerous Brazilian friends.

Lois understood that a single person has to have close friends. While a married person has a mate and often children, the single missionary naturally turns to local Christians for fellowship.

At the end of that first term, a missionary woman told her, "Lois, I wasn't in favor of your coming, but I am so glad you're here. Please hurry back after furlough." Three others who had been hesitant about her coming are today some of Lois' close friends. Such positive encouragement, as she departed the Amazon after her first term, gave Lois an overwhelming desire to hurry back to the Amazon.

Since her arrival in Brazil in 1967, Lois Wantoch has served the Lord effectively. She is loved and appreciated by missionaries and national believers alike. For five years, she worked in Santo Antônio do Içá. Lois turned a tool shop in the backyard of the mission property into a clinic. She diagnosed and treated all types of patients who came from the town and the outlying areas. She delivered babies in the homes, on wood floors under mosquito netting. She extracted badly decayed teeth, and tended medical emergencies to the best of her ability. She was distressed and frustrated when some of her patients died for lack of adequate medical facilities. Lois began to realize the great need for a mission hospital in this area of the Amazon.

It's a myth to believe that single women missionaries can't be successful servants of the Lord Jesus Christ on the Amazon.

The Amazon is a tough place to evangelize. Alas, for the golden days of William Carey and Adoniram Judson. Are missionaries of their caliber left? Oh, for iron-souled soldiers of the cross to reach this area. Is God making missionaries like He used to?

MYTH NO. 4

God Isn't Making Missionaries Like He Used To

"The glorious days of Carey and Judson will never return."

Jack, a typical American boy growing up in Willoughby, Ohio, heard the gospel week in and week out. He sat through many salvation messages, never feeling any personal conviction.

Summer camp at Stony Glen (Ohio) was a family ritual, so in 1954, during his ninth year, Jack was there. Camp closed on Sunday. During a Bible session in which the camp counselor was talking about something else, he off-handedly asked Jack, "Are you saved?" Struck by the question, Jack answered, "I think so . . . I'm not sure . . . No." During the moment it took to form his response, God convicted Jack of sin. He realized he had never received Christ as Savior. When the teacher suggested they look at some Bible verses, Jack said, "I know the verses. I just need to pray." Right then, he became a Christian. Four decades later, Jack said, "I can still remember, even as a nine-year-old, the feeling of my sin burden being lifted."

During his junior-high years, Jack continued to attend church and Sunday school, and read the Bible. But his heart was not in it. In junior high, he started hanging around with an ungodly crowd, and had an unsaved girlfriend.

In tenth grade, a friend from Jack's home church invited him to a club called HiBA (High School Born-Againers). The club's purpose is to train Christian high schoolers to be missionaries in their own schools. The program included daily devotions, Scripture memory work, finding God's will, and witnessing. Jack began to grow spiritually and to pray earnestly about God's will for his life.

In Willowick, Ohio, near Jack's hometown of Willoughby, another teen also grew up attending church. At one point, along with others, she was ushered before the church and introduced as having been saved and, therefore, a candidate for baptism.

But Sandy was frustrated by her attempts to live a good life. She knew that she was not "making it." Seeing God as a stern Judge, Sandy began toying with the thought, *Since I am going to hell for a little sin, I might as well enjoy myself and go to hell for a lot of sin.* A friend invited her to HiBA. Since Jack organized transportation to those meetings, he made sure that Sandy had a ride.

While attending a youth rally, Sandy was impressed with the emphasis on God's love. As the preacher spoke from 1 John 4:10, Sandy realized for the first time that God loved her. That evening she accepted Christ as her Savior, finally experiencing His love.

At the start of Jack's senior year in high school, HiBA held a missionary rally in a church in the greater Cleveland area, with hundreds of high school students and lots of displays. One display focused on Pakistan's need for medical missionaries. Jack said, "That impressed me. I had never thought of anything like that. With medical missions on my mind, I went into the meeting that night. I still remember the message, based on Ezekiel 33:1–16, about the watchman on the wall. We were challenged to go wherever God wanted us to go, and do whatever God wanted us to do."

Sincerely considering that challenge, Jack noticed a display that listed missionary opportunities. Running down the list, he thought, *Missionary? Okay, I could do that. Pastor? Okay, I could see myself being a pastor.* At the bottom of the list Jack noticed "doctor." Being a doctor was unattractive because he couldn't imagine enjoying medicine. He went forward in church to say that he would go anywhere, but he really was saying, *I know God is going to send me to some jungle. I'll do anything but be a doctor.*

During the next three weeks, Jack struggled with the anything/anywhere question, knowing he hadn't committed himself to God completely. Matthew 28:19–20 burned into his brain. It became increasingly obvious that God was leading him to become a doctor. Drawing on fledgling negotiating skills—which would later be finely honed—the young man set two criteria: God would have to open the opportunities for medical training, and God would have to give him enjoyment in being a doctor. God graciously answered both abundantly, and provided a call through Joshua 1:9: *Be strong and of good courage; be not afraid, neither be thou dismayed, for the Lord thy God is with thee withersoever thou goest.*

At that same mission rally, independent of Jack, Sandy went forward to commit her life to missions. Romans 10:14 was instrumental in directing Sandy: ". . . how shall they believe in Him of whom they have not heard."

Later, reconstructing a mosaic of that evening, Jack and Sandy confirmed they were to marry and go to the mission field together. God had His man: Jack Sorg; and Jack had his companion, Sandy.

Preparation for Service

Bible college at Bob Jones University for both (where they crammed a major into one year) was followed by nursing school for Sandy at Mt. Sinai Hospital School of Nursing in Cleveland, and medical school at Case Western Reserve in Cleveland for Jack. Next, Jack entered general surgery training in Grady Memorial and Piedmont hospitals near Atlanta. Because he didn't plan to practice general surgery in the States, Jack took elective courses outside the general surgery curriculum: dermatology, pediatrics, obstetrics, and anesthesia. While his colleagues were honing their skills for specialization, he was looking at the broad spectrum of human need for general health outside the United States.

In 1975, partway through general surgery training, the Sorgs wanted to get a firsthand look at medical missions. Two years after the book *Daktar/Diplomat in Bangladesh* was published, Jack and Sandy moved into the home of the author, Dr. Viggo Olsen, in Malumghat, Bangladesh, to work at Memorial Christian Hospital. Reading Vic's personal copy of the book, interacting with the people in the book, and being on-site was an enormously profitable time of seeing medical missions in action. The Sorgs served at Malumghat for six months, as God continued to prepare them for future service.

After Bangladesh, Jack invested three years of general surgery training at Piedmont Hospital in Atlanta. Allowed by the hospital to treat patients free of charge with top-quality medical care, Jack was able to help missionaries. Calling from Brazil, ABWE missionary Hank Scheltema asked, "Could I come for a much-needed operation and get treatment for other medical problems?"

While Hank was a patient in Jack's care, the veteran missionary told the young doctor about the Amazon jungle and its possibilities for medical missions.

Over the next two years, the Sorgs continued to pray about God's direction for their lives. Jack talked to missionaries and studied mission literature. Three questions confronted the couple as they sought God's direction.

1. Should they be in an itinerant ministry where they would travel overland or by river, village to village, or would a permanent location advance the kingdom more? Since the Lord had led Jack into surgical training, a permanent location seemed reasonable.
2. Did they want an outpatient clinic or an actual hospital that could care for more serious illnesses and provide both inpatient and outpatient care? Again, in light of Jack's expertise in surgery, the hospital-based approach made sense.
3. Into which type of medical missions did they want to pour their lives? The Association of Baptists for World

Evangelism (ABWE) has two types of medical missions:

- A hospital in a country where there is active church planting. In this case, the hospital feeds the already active church-planting ministry, lending credibility that flows out of the loving, self-sacrificing service of a Christian hospital. In the Philippines and Togo, West Africa, hospitals support previously initiated church-planting efforts and put the character of God on display. Local people can see God loves them and has sent these medical workers to help them.
- A hospital in a country such as Bangladesh or The Gambia serves as the main spiritual trailblazer. Churches grow up around the hospital as a result of the loving care provided at the hospital. In this second approach to evangelism and church planting, doctors and nurses may be the spiritual commandos, and church planters follow. In Bangladesh, church planters worked in the country for some years before the hospital existed, but the hospital enhanced church planting. In such situations, government authorities and local people tolerate the presence of foreigners in exchange for the medical help provided.

Although it was a hard decision, the Sorgs felt their skills and interests could be best used through the first approach: a hospital working in the midst of church planters. The Sorgs opted for the Philippines/Togo approach, near established groups of believers in a large area that still needed to be evangelized.

Veteran missionary Hank Scheltema painted the Amazon to Jack and Sandy: 500 miles of river, covered by a handful of church planters, in which the town of Santo Antônio do Içá was centrally located. There was a small church, surrounded by a multitude of unreached towns and villages, with no hospital and little government interest in building one. Just what the Sorgs were looking for!

After his surgery in 1977, Hank Scheltema returned to Brazil and led the field council to extend an invitation to the Sorgs to survey the upper Amazon area to determine the feasibility of a medical work. Though she was seven months pregnant with their third child, Sandy took part in the survey trip. Santo Antônio do Içá ideally suited the Sorgs. The town is located in the midst of ABWE's Amazon church planting effort, with Brazilian and Ticuna Indian churches nearby, but unlimited evangelism opportunities in villages within a 100-mile radius.

Looking for confirmation of their choice of location, Jack and Sandy Sorg consulted the Brazilian Secretary of Health for the state of Amazonas, without revealing their own preference. The official volunteered that Santo Antônio do Içá would be the best site for a hospital, since the government had no plans to build one there. Additional confirmation came through praying and Bible reading, focusing on Isaiah 6:8–9a: "Also I heard the voice of the Lord, saying, Whom shall I send, and who will go for us? Then said I, Here am I; send me. And he said, Go, and tell this people." In July 1978, the Sorgs committed to go to the Amazon under the auspices of ABWE. But someone else also had plans for Dr. Jack Sorg.

Two Masters

As a member of the U.S. Army Reserves, Jack had been guaranteed a deferment of active duty until he finished surgical training in 1978. Writing the military about a change of address, Dr. Sorg included a note that he was now ordained as a Baptist minister, and was planning to be a missionary. He asked if that would change his status in the Army. The young doctor wanted to resign so he could start with the mission, but was scheduled for active duty with the Army in July of 1978.

For months, the military did not reply. Finally, in the fall of 1977, a captain from the Pentagon called. Jack recalls, "My first thought was, I must have done something terribly wrong for an officer from the Pentagon to call me." The military officer acknowledged receipt of Dr. Sorg's letter months before, and said he was "working on it," so Jack had to wait for the captain's response.

Three months later, in January of 1978, the captain called again. Apologizing that his response had taken so long, he spoke of difficulty in finding the regulation that applied to Jack. Canvassing his friends, the captain had dug up an army regulation stating that an officer who is ordained by a recognized religious group could tender his resignation.

Jack explained that he had been ordained within the General Association of Regular Baptist Churches, and that he felt called to missionary work in Brazil. But he also said that if summoned for active duty, he would serve his country, since he was not a conscientious objector.

By the end of May, Jack had received orders for his final medical exam, and had been told where to appear on July 1, 1978. Destination? Ankara, Turkey. Then on the last day of May, the Sorgs received an envelope with one sheet of paper in it: Dr. Jack Sorg's honorable discharge from the Armed Services of the United States. The Sorgs never met the captain in the Pentagon, but God worked through him. Jack explained, "We shifted our thinking away from Turkey. I had the discharge paper framed and kept it on the wall for a long time; very handy in case the Army Military Police showed up, wondering why I wasn't on active duty in Turkey."

After Jack completed his studies in general surgery, the Sorgs began their pre-field ministry in 1979, speaking in churches and schools. They left for language school in Brazil in 1980.

Amazing Provision

When God is going to do something in keeping with His character, He often allows huge obstacles to cloud the horizon of those He uses. Everyone agreed that a hospital was to be built. But how? The new missionary doctor had no money. Still largely unknown and without a proven record, the Sorgs wondered how to proceed.

It was the spring of 1979. Pastor Robert Spradling of the Bible

Center Church in Charleston, West Virginia, called ABWE and said, "We are between building projects and would like to do a missions emphasis. Are you now building anything for which we could give money?" Hearing of the proposed hospital on the Amazon, the pastor was interested. "How much would your young doctor need to build a hospital?" Pastor Spradling inquired.

Answering that question was difficult because of unknown variables: the size of the building, construction material (wood or masonry), distance from the source of supply, and the fluctuating purchasing power of the American dollar. Since Pastor Spradling seemed to want a sizable project, Jack suggested that a $10,000 gift would be wonderful.

Pastor Spradling asked, "Is that enough to build a hospital?"

In a scene reminding us of Abraham talking with God in Genesis 18:22–33, Jack upped the amount to $20,000. Out-Abrahaming our doctor, Pastor Spradling asked, "Would $20,000 *finish* a hospital down there?"

"No, we would need more. It would take $40,000 to get a basic building up," Jack answered.

That amount was more in line with what the people of Bible Center Church had in mind. But could they do it? One church? In one, four-day missions conference? Even in this church of 600 members, achieving their goal would rank among the outstanding investments of the church's life.

When the project was presented, the Holy Spirit created a climate of adventurous giving. People dreamed of what a hospital on the Amazon could do to love people to Christ. Excitement built. Dr. Sorg was a bit nervous about their high goal.

The first night, believers gave $37,000; within touching distance of their goal! They had saved their nickels, dimes, and extra dollar bills. Some had sold items and given the money that first night. Some business people bargained with God: "Lord, if You bless my venture, all the money will go to the hospital." Witnessing the sacrificial giving of some, others were prompted by the

Holy Spirit to give. By the next evening, over $47,000 had been contributed. Though over the goal, people came back night after night, giving yet again!

Pastor Spradling reported, "Over 160 people gave and no single gift was larger than $2,000. We were touched by the participation of our handicapped members. A blind woman living on a fixed income gave $500. A young man who is crippled gave $260. A man with hydrocephalus contributed 5,000 dimes. Many elderly people gave amounts of $100 or more. What an enormous blessing this turned out to be for our entire church."

In accord with 2 Corinthians 9:7, this was *hilarious* giving. By the end of the four days, church members had given $53,000. Other gifts, and interest from a four-year delay until building, brought the total to $63,000.

That's a heady and intoxicating experience for a church. A grand thing when the living God moves upon the minds and wills of His own.

A Helper in the Task: William D. Hawley, Jr.

Bill Hawley was born in West Virginia and saved at the age of 14 after hearing the gospel message at a tent meeting. After high school, Bill attended Bob Jones University to major in Bible, then attended medical school at West Virginia University. He married Patricia in 1966, four years before his graduation from WVU.

Following medical school, Bill served his internship, spent three years in the Navy, and entered private medical practice. During this time he and Patty remained active in their local church, open to God's leading in their lives. After hearing ABWE missionary Gene Gurganus speak at their church, the Hawleys again asked God for specific direction for their future. Shortly thereafter, Bill read the book *Daktar,* and the Hawleys attended ABWE's conference in Bermuda. During those days God called them into career missionary service.

Bill and Patty were accepted by ABWE in 1978. They were set

to leave for Brazil in the summer of 1980, but were delayed by continued lack of response for resident visas from the Brazilian government. While the Hawleys waited for the imminent arrival of their visas, which they needed to have in hand before departing from Greenville, South Carolina, they were actively involved in the Amazon work. Dave Kriegel, a commercial builder friend from Greenville, agreed to live in Santo Antônio do Içá for a year to oversee the hospital construction. Architect Jerry Peifer, another friend of the Hawleys, traveled to Brazil in October of 1980 and spent 10 days gathering information on the availability and prices of building materials. Jerry was then able to revise his plans for the hospital building, based on his on-site survey.

During the unexpected delay, Bill observed a dentist friend at work to learn basic dentistry. He also attended a six-week tropical medical course with the U.S. Army. The Hawleys collected donations of equipment (such as a serometer, which would perform 20 different laboratory tests), and began learning Portuguese, until Bill and Patty and their children, Jonathan, Sarah, and David, were able to depart for Brazil in September of 1981 with tourist visas in hand.

Although their first year in Brazil was spent studying the language in Manaus, Bill was involved in a church planting work started by Ed Blakeslee. Bill helped lead singing, taught a Bible study for young people, and went on visitation. Individual Bible studies with new converts rounded out Bill's early responsibilities.

Bill wrote of a humorous Sunday service that took place in the summer of 1982. "We had about 18 in the poor old car—quite close fellowship. Shortly after we started the service, the electricity went out. We finally got some candles lit and the confusion more or less settled down. Son David held a candle over my Bible while I preached on the prodigal son. There was a brief diversion when one little boy's hair caught on fire and our daughter, Sarah, smacked it out with her hand. But when the invitation was given, one woman lifted her hand. That's what it's all about, isn't it?"

It wasn't until June of 1982 that FUNAI (the Brazilian agency established by the federal government to aid and protect the indigenous peoples of the country) approved the hospital project, which in turn resulted in the granting of residential visas for the entire team. The Brazilian government told the Hawleys to return to the United States to pick up the visas. However, when they arrived at the Brazilian consulate in Atlanta, they faced additional setbacks in getting their visas. The Hawleys used the unexpected six-week delay to collect and pack equipment to be shipped to the hospital. While Jack Sorg and his family moved to Santo Antônio do Içá to begin the initial oversight of construction, Bill and Patty completed language study.

By November of 1983, the Hawleys were looking at purchasing a boat to use in medical/evangelistic outreach from Santo Antônio. One year later, the boat had arrived and was in use. Bill and Patty were planning their strategy for outreach along the river. In November of 1984, the Hawley family had to make a quick trip to Colombia to resolve their ongoing visa problem. The medical work was, according to Bill, "small-scale" while hospital construction continued, but resulted in good personal contacts. The church in Santo Antônio was finally pastored by a Brazilian and had around 200 in attendance each Sunday. Bill was especially encouraged by the opportunities to conduct Bible studies with new converts.

The Hawleys' residence near the hospital was completed in June of 1985, and on September 22, 1985, Amazonas Baptist Hospital officially opened. The medical work was moved from the local state health clinic to the hospital one week later. The early weeks in the hospital were given to setting up and putting into use the laboratory and X-ray equipment. Outpatient attendance ran 20–25 people per day, with inpatient care for one to five patients. Bill continued to teach the teen Sunday school class, help with preaching occasionally, and disciple new converts.

Bill wrote in 1988 and 1989 of several severe medical cases that resulted in personal decisions for salvation.

- Pedro, a 17-year-old boy, had an accident with fireworks and had to have large portions of three fingers amputated. "Although he left the hospital with a serious handicap," Bill wrote, "he trusted Christ as his Savior while he was with us."
- The hospital's laundress gave her husband a shot of penicillin for his back strain. He promptly responded with a severe allergic reaction, arriving at the hospital with no blood pressure and a rapidly fading pulse. Emergency measures resuscitated her husband and the shock of that near-death experience impressed him with his need of salvation.
- Alcivane, a 10-year-old girl, arrived at the hospital with a broken thigh bone. The Hawleys' daughter, Sarah, led her to the Lord during Christmas vacation.
- Raimundo prayed to receive Christ as Savior before leaving the hospital after recovering from congestive heart failure and pneumonia.

August 1989 found Bill Hawley and Jack Sorg overwhelmed with more patients than ever. Bill reported progress in the local church under the ministry of a new Brazilian pastor, with professions of faith and increased participation by the young people.

In the spring of 1990, Bill and Patty rejoiced in the results of their weekend riverboat outreach. On one occasion, they visited house to house in Tonantins, meeting in almost every dwelling someone who had been treated at the Amazonas Baptist Hospital. Bill preached to an attentive group of around 60 on the subject, "How can you escape the judgment of hell?" He also preached to a newly formed congregation of about 30, where two young people made decisions for Christ.

The Hawleys worked at Amazonas Baptist Hospital until family health matters required them to return to the United States in 1990. Bill served as choir director and adult Bible teacher in his home church, and continued to travel to the Amazon every few years to serve short term at the hospital he helped to start.

In October of 1997, Bill was diagnosed with an inoperable, rapidly growing brain tumor. He wrote to a friend, "Let's just let God be God." A few months before his death, Bill was able to make a final visit to Santo Antônio, where the Brazilians held a beautiful ceremony honoring his service to their community. He was deeply loved by those he served. On August 13, 1998, Bill was ushered into the presence of the Lord he loved so well.

Other physicians and surgeons served in a long- or short-term capacity, but Jack Sorg and Bill Hawley were involved in the initial phases, and are remembered as the founders of the Amazonas Baptist Hospital.

Jack and Bill prove that God ***is*** *making missionaries like He used to. They and the other members of the team God assembled to present Himself to the people of the Amazon region show their love is obvious, their commitment outspoken, and their dedication well known. Their motives are right. Certainly they must be free to serve. Right?*

MYTH NO. 5

Politics Don't Impact Our Missionaries

"Brazil will give us visas and medical licenses right away so we can serve the Brazilian people."

Control of many Latin American countries shifts between the state church, civil government, and the military, each enjoying the upper hand until upstaged. The year 1964 was no different from other years, since the big three—government, military, and church—were contending for power. Unknown to most in the country, however, the balance of power was about to shift cataclysmically.

Of the three contenders, the church has dominated over the centuries. Brazil has been a religious country for the last 400 years, with the Roman Catholic Church holding a virtual monopoly. As the official state religion, Roman Catholicism enjoyed protection and approval. Church-related building permits came easily; church-sanctioned politicians gained the votes of the faithful; and business deals moved quickly for Roman Catholics, while others experienced endless red tape and bureaucratic frustration.

In some areas of Brazil, the persecution suffered by evangelical Christians was led by Roman Catholic authorities, and included stones thrown at evangelicals during public preaching, or missionaries being told they were not welcome in a given community.

But in 1964, a new player appeared on the horizon. The leftist movement was gaining ground fast. Because they won the national elections, they were poised to take over Brazil.

One goal of the leftist party was to break the official link between the church and the government. While still a huge voting block in national politics, the church no longer had a direct, iron-clad link to power.

At this strategic moment, the military (traditionally conservative and strongly anti-Communist) launched a coup and overthrew the elected government, successfully establishing military control that lasted for 20 years. Gradually the military turned power back to the civil government.

What was the attitude of the civil government when it returned to power in 1984? Happy to be out from under the thumb of the church, the new civil government was pleased to continue the official break with the Roman Catholic Church. Lip service to the church has continued, while civil authorities enjoy their liberation from centuries of dominance.

Though rural areas resisted the new freedom of religion laws, Bible-believing Christians made significant gains in the years since the 1964 coup. Some concessions previously given only to the Roman Catholic Church were thereafter also extended to the evangelicals. In some instances where the Catholic church wanted land for a Church, the community also set aside land for Baptists, Pentecostals, and other groups.

Members of evangelical churches entered government service, further creating a climate receptive to biblical Christianity. Of all the Latin American countries, evangelical gains have been the greatest in Brazil. The town of Tabatinga even has a Baptist mayor!

Illustrations of New Religious Liberties

With a 300-year-old archdiocese, local Roman Catholic loyalty was well established in the town of São Paulo de Olivência. Attempting to preach there prior to 1964, ABWE missionaries were run out of town. But with the new legal freedoms trickling into the remote interior, in 1988 the missionaries were actually invited to São Paulo de Olivência and encouraged to build a church.

In the town of Amaturá, the Roman Catholic Church owned a block of land, taking up—literally—the whole middle of the village within one block of the waterfront. Half the town had developed on either side of the church's property. Anyone wanting contact with the other half of the village had to walk the several blocks of undeveloped land in the middle. A footpath of about 200 yards connected the two sides, but there was no road to accommodate vehicles. Tensions mounted about the unnecessary cleavage: the civil government wanted to build a road to connect the two sides of the town, and the church resisted giving up any of its property. One time while the priest was out of town, the mayor called in a bulldozer and constructed a road connecting the two arms of the town. Such action would have been unheard of prior to 1964.

Consider two examples of politics that impact Amazon missions: the visa juggernaut and the medical license saga.

Visa Juggernaut and Military Power

When problems and delays arose in trying to enter Brazil on a permanent visa, the Sorgs opted to go to Manaus on a tourist visa. During 1981, eight more ABWE missionaries arrived in Manaus for language study. Those were heady times of spiritual excitement; progress was in the air.

An unsaved Brazilian landlord, whose wife was a believer, took a liking to the missionaries. Interested in the Sorgs' housing needs, he offered to buy a house nearby. Instead of paying rent, the American doctor could make repairs on the house, using the rent money for needed materials.

In the next two-and-one-half years, the Sorgs paid no rent money, but doubled the size of the house and installed electrical wiring and air conditioning. Walls were moved, and windows installed. The landlord was happy to receive free labor. The Sorgs had a good house and gained construction experience, which God knew they would need later.

In Manaus, the ten ABWE missionaries worked on studying Portuguese and trying to obtain visas, the former easier than the latter. Language skills grew, while the visa process sank in government bureaucracy. Months passed before the missionaries concluded that more action was needed. Various individuals visited the visa office in Brasilia (the capital) several times, to no avail. Their paperwork had, indeed, gotten lost. Through Christian friends of other Christian friends who worked in the State Department, the paper trail was traced to a file cabinet in an office of Brasilia. Officials were sitting on it, and a special agreement had to be reached before permission to live in Santo do Antônio Içá would be granted.

Setting to work in earnest on the visa trail, the missionaries made slow progress. Flying 1,100 miles south from Manaus to Brasilia and back was expensive, but with visas hanging in the balance, it was worth it. When the agreement was finalized, mission officials signed it. The next step involved getting signatures from FUNAI, after which the visas were to be sent back to the Brazilian State Department.

At this point, officials declared, "We want to change the agreement." Returning to the capital, Jack Sorg navigated through government bureaucracy all the way to the top man: a military colonel, since the government was under military control in 1983. Explaining the situation to him, Dr. Sorg appealed to proceed with the agreed-upon document and negotiate changes in future agreements. Thinking that reasonable, the colonel pulled out the documents, signed them, and sent them off. Wonderful!

Wow, thought the missionaries, *the big barrier is gone*. Not so. Another army colonel, the head of the State Department, held up the paperwork. Even worse, the missionaries couldn't make an appointment to see the State Department head.

To add to the confusion, a government department was erroneously informed that the missionaries were working and earning money that should go to Brazilians. Because of that, the missionaries' tourist visas would no longer be renewed.

The missionaries' initial discouragement gave way to the recognition that God now *had to do something* in the next month or ABWE would have to abandon the hope of a hospital on the Amazon.

This was both a desperate and exciting moment in the missionaries' lives. Desperate in that so much had been risked to get this far, exciting in that if God wanted a hospital on the upper Amazon, He would have to do it. There was nothing else human skill, diligence, effort, or creativity could do. Dr. Sorg said, "We were praising God because this situation was, finally, humanly impossible. We had done all anyone could. There was nothing to do but continue in prayer. God had to act."

Enter God via the unsaved but sympathetic landlord. He told the missionaries about a distant relative who worked in a high government position and might be able to help. Reluctance to working through unsaved friends yielded to, "Okay, Lord. You are in charge; do it any way You see fit." There was nothing else to try.

The landlord never said what position his cousin had, just that he had a "very good job." Arriving in the capital city of Brasilia, ABWE missionaries Ed Blakeslee and Jack Sorg found that the relative was one of the top five advisors to the military president of Brazil, and worked in the Palácio, the Brazilian "White House."

To the Brazilian White House

The Brazilian advisor talked to the missionaries for five minutes, asking some polite questions. He obviously already knew their problems, what they were doing, and what he was going to do about it. He said they needed to speak to the colonel in charge of visas and passports. The Americans responded, "Yes, sir. That is an excellent idea." The Holy Spirit enabled them *not* to add, *We've been trying for the last year and a half to do exactly that!*

The advisor continued, "I will call him just now and make an appointment for the three of us." That was equivalent to the White House calling the State Department and asking for an appointment. The only appropriate response was, "Yes, sir! When?" The presidential advisor and the State Department head agreed upon that afternoon, apologizing to the missionaries that the meeting could not take place sooner.

Returning that afternoon in the advisor's limousine, the three men met the colonel. After introductions, the advisor put his hand on Dr. Jack's shoulder and said to the government official, "My friends need visas to come into Brazil. Can you help us?"

The colonel vacillated for a moment. Then he said he would be glad to process the visa for the advisor's American friends. Apologetic that he was deeply engrossed in another important matter, he explained that he would not be able to get to the job for 24 hours. The presidential advisor turned to Jack and said, "Well, is 24 hours all right with you?"

Dr. Sorg paused for a moment. Years of frustration had been invested to arrive at this moment. Was the 24 hours just another ploy? Dare he allow his long-awaited leverage to slip away? How demanding could he be? Not very.

"One more day would be fine," he answered.

True to his word, less than 24 hours later, the presidential advisor called Jack and Ed to his office. Then, from the Palácio, in the advisor's limo, the three men again went to see the colonel at the State Department.

Stacked on his desk were ten beautiful visas. Next to the visas lay an accumulated stack of paperwork one-and-one-half feet high—the missionaries' efforts to secure visas.

"Your permanent visas have been granted," announced the colonel.

By law, long-term visas had to be picked up at a Brazilian consulate outside of the country. The colonel couldn't simply hand them over. Still wary and concerned about bureaucratic loopholes, Jack asked, "When will the visas be at the consulates?"

"Ah, yes, wait a minute." The colonel left the room. Returning he said, "They are on the teletype machines to the consulates now. By the time you get back to your hotel, the consulates will already be advised of your visas. You can pick them up any time." The procedure required that two one-year visas be given before a person was allowed a permanent visa. The purpose of the one-year visa is to permit the Brazilian government to see if the person is really who he says he is, and if he is doing what he said he was in Brazil to do.

This remarkable turn of events—since this advisor to the Brazilian military president was the only civilian advisor and is staunchly Roman Catholic—shows God's mighty power! As Jack and Ed departed that day, the advisor pulled Jack aside and said, "I have one request for you. Please stay out of politics."

The field council minutes of August 26, 1982, add this note: "The government in general is favorable to evangelical missionaries, realizing their great contribution to social stability (in a country whose motto is *Order and Progress*). Missionaries who preach the Bible are appreciated. Missionaries who work for social and government change are not. This difference in missionaries will be a chief criterion for renewal of the one-year visa."

Jack and his family returned to the United States to get their temporary visas, stayed about three months, then returned to Brazil. The other eight missionaries also left Brazil to pick up the temporary visas which they had been seeking for three years. Another two years passed before permanent visas were granted in 1985. God solved the visa juggernaut.

Medical License Saga

As the visa saga was taking place, Jack Sorg applied for medical certification in 1982, while the Sorgs were still in the United

States. His being fully approved and licensed to practice medicine in America didn't mean he would be accepted *carte blanche* on the Amazon.

The licensing of doctors was controlled by the federal government through a special mandate to each state university. Jack applied to the Amazon State University. In 1982, with the assistance of the vice president of the university, a man named Dr. Rocha, Dr. Sorg's Brazilian medical certification was granted in a matter of months. All that remained was for the university president to sign the certificate and for Dr. Sorg to pick it up in Manaus.

Two problems interfered, however, between Jack and the coveted certification. First, the medical license could not be granted to the holder of a temporary tourist visa. Jack had to obtain a one-year resident visa. Using his temporary tourist visa, Dr. Jack had gone in and out of the country repeatedly to try to obtain a one-year visa. It took another year for the visa situation to be resolved, so this was a "hurry up and wait" situation. Jack had rushed to complete the medical license process while the friendly university vice-president was in power. But everything came to a standstill as he waited another year for God to resolve the visa situation.

In 1983, one-year visa in hand, Dr. Sorg set off to Manaus on the very day he received the resident visa, only to meet the second—more daunting—obstacle. The university's policies had changed, making it more difficult for Jack to gain approval of his U.S. medical degree. Jack reported, "I discovered my medical diploma, which was in the new president's office, needing only his signature, had been thrown in the trash about two weeks before the resident visa was granted because of the length of time that had elapsed since my original application."

Since Dr. Sorg was already practicing medicine, and enjoyed the unofficial approval of the health authorities, why bother with the hassle of certification? What could be gained?

- First, it was the law. In Brazil, compliance was mandatory, not optional.
- Second, without a certified doctor on site, national registration of the hospital was withheld.
- Third, while unregistered, the hospital could not advertise for help and had to keep a low profile.
- Fourth, without hospital registration, certain medicines were unobtainable or difficult to bring into Brazil.
- Fifth, an uncertified doctor could not sign official documents such as birth or death certificates.
- Sixth, patients could not be charged for services. While the amounts generated are minimal, paying something causes the patient to value the care and treatment provided.
- Seventh—and most significant—without a certified doctor, the Amazonas Baptist Hospital was a legal non-entity. Though supported—unofficially—by state health authorities, the hospital was in legal limbo—it did not exist. This limited the full potential of the mission hospital ministry.

These reasons made it attractive to stay on the scent of official recognition.

The university president's office informed Dr. Sorg that he should start the process all over again. Providentially, a friend salvaged the paperwork from the president's wastebasket, so at least Jack had a head start. Two years of prayer went by before authorities looked at his re-submitted documents. The officials claimed they sent a letter to inform him of additional documentation still required. Dr. Sorg never received the letter. Three years later, a photocopy of the letter was found.

Two more years passed before the needed documents could be collected. They then gathered dust on someone's desk in the bowels of the bureaucracy.

But God has His own timing. By 1993, ten years into Dr. Sorg's new certification process, Brazil's national government was calling for upgraded health care for the interior. When the Brazilian government wanted to upgrade health care on the upper Amazon River, they sponsored a conference in Manaus. The purpose of the conference was to paint the Amazon in attractive colors to recruit doctors for those communities. How many doctors came to the conference? None. How many doctors were successfully recruited for Amazon villages? None. The government conference, designed to attract doctors to the upper river areas, failed totally.

Pressured to streamline and reorganize the foreign graduate diploma process, the medical establishment at the Manaus university finally responded. A friend of a friend of Dr. Sorg got his paperwork re-introduced to this updated system.

After he had completed the required three months of clinical work, Dr. Jack Sorg received his official medical certification. With characteristic good humor, Jack dismissed the 12-year saga with, "The paperwork could have been taped on the back of a turtle with a broken leg and gotten to the president's desk faster." With certification in hand, Dr. Jack Sorg was free to love the Brazilian people through healing their bodies.

Politics don't impact our missionaries is a myth. But God rules and overrules on all frontiers of our lives to advance His work. One such frontier is the North American misconception that missionaries are destroying the culture of otherwise happy natives.

MYTH NO. 6

Missionaries Destroy Native Culture

"You missionaries are cultural imperialists who are bothering happy natives."

"Sit down! Yes, sit down right here," the village captain (mayor) directed. So ABWE missionaries Tom and Beth Peace sat down at the table of Manuel Flores, the captain of the Ticuna Indian village of Betânia, and his wife, Maria. The captain was eager to report to his friends Tom and Beth a conversation he had with government officials.

"Anthropologists told us, 'You don't have to let those missionaries in. They aren't helping you. We can make the missionaries leave.'

"I asked them, 'Where were you when we needed help? When we had no rights and no others were helping us? When non-Indian peoples wanted to steal our fields, take our money, get us drunk, and rape our women? The missionaries love us and take care of us! Time after time Eduardo [ABWE missionary Lindsay Edward Harrell] and his wife, Jean, came in the middle of the night and took care of sick people. If we could pay for the medicine, we did. If we couldn't, he would give us the medicine. He is a father to me!'

"I told those anthropologists, 'As long as I am alive, the missionaries can be here.'"

This was the mayor's strong reply to the idea that missionaries are enemies of native culture.

The accusation that missionaries are destroying native culture comes in various forms, but the attitude is, *Why don't you leave those happy natives alone? How intolerant and culturally imperialistic can you be? Who are you to impose yourself and your religion on others?* Let's talk reality here.

Separation of Church and State

While some missionaries entered primitive cultures and pushed colonialism, most missionaries have tried not to do that. Most desire to respect the music, marriage customs, and language of the indigenous people. They do, however, seek to teach about the God of the Bible, and the biblical way of salvation.

It's ironic that the same individuals who seek to protect the Indians also cause change in what they attempt to protect. Consider what happens by the simple, humanitarian act of providing free medicine to Indians. Dependency is created by such supposedly neutral contacts. The introduction of modern medicine challenges the authority of the witch doctor by putting modern medicine in competition with his healing powers.

When ABWE missionaries arrive in a village, among the first questions asked is, "What medicine do you have for us?" Villages are often hit hard by dysentery, malaria, measles, and worms. Once, Beth Peace visited a village so overcome by malaria that not one person was sufficiently healthy to paddle out for help. Suppose God had not sent Beth to that village? Many would have died.

Change is inevitable, however it arrives.

Isolation Is No Longer Possible

Once an Indian tribe is discovered, it is no longer totally isolated. Changes may come subtly, but they come. As contacts expand, the tribe learns more about the newcomers' value system, customs, beliefs, abilities, technology, and power. The less sophisticated the belief system and lifestyle of the tribe, the more easily the tribe is changed. The extent and rapidity of the change depend on the strength, sophistication, and size of the tribe—a stronger, more complex, and larger tribe takes longer to change.

The White Man's Sins and Technology

The government has a good motive in wanting to keep the white man's diseases from tribal people. Reality shows it's too late for that isolation. Often, it is the Indian himself who paddles out of the jungle to seek material goods. Tribal people are exposed to the good and bad of Western culture. Having taken the initiative for themselves, can we then isolate them, withholding medicines and other help?

It is true that tribes do adopt some of the white man's worst elements. Our vices, such as alcohol, also ensnare them. While our sins are quickly adopted, since the Indians are sinners like the rest of us, our faith is not so readily absorbed. Add to that the greed of selfish men who seek the land on which the politically powerless Indian lives. While it may appear that the Indian would be better off without the white man, let's not hang all the guilt on missionaries.

20th Century Conquistadors

Businessmen, combing the globe, are going to invade whatever domains exist to achieve their goals. History tells us they will exploit without appropriate compensation. Since that is a certainty, it is a matter of whether such primitive peoples are exposed to this type of 20th-century *conquistador* only, or whether at least some people offer genuine help. Better some missionaries and others who really care, than only the 20th-century *conquistadors*.

Government agencies seek to limit, or at least carefully control, contact with the indigenous peoples. Some officials are adamant that the tribes' contact with Christianity is the main culprit in corrupting the natives. Looking at a few missions, they may find some justification, but in most cases they are misguided.

The Missionaries' Goal

Evangelical missionaries seek to equip individuals to face the difficulties, differences, and deceptions of this life through saving faith in Jesus Christ. Trust in the Lord and scriptural truth give the wisdom needed to face both tribal and civilized life.

Biblical missionaries seek to aid the Indians with the most helpful aspects of our culture—medicine and tools—without dismantling the tribal culture, or removing the people from it. Those missionaries must (and do) give local people principles that help them to grow *in their own society*, no matter who makes contact with them.

The environmentalists' purist approach is philosophically untenable and realistically unattainable. The main difficulty the missionary faces in his contact with primitive cultures is that any Christian approach is viewed by some as being wrong, shortsighted, and politically incorrect. Bible-believing missionaries are judged by the world's flawed standards.

What about the Brazilians themselves? Do they welcome missionaries to their land?

THE STORY OF ABWE'S MEDICAL WORK

ON THE AMAZON

JUNGLE MYTHS

Nurse Sherry Skirrow on duty.

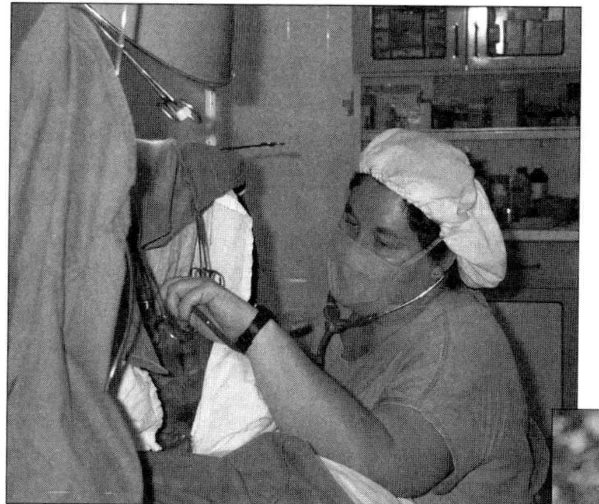

Tom Peace, traveling on the Amazon by motorboat.

Above:
Indian hunter with his blowgun and arrow.

Left:
Initial dedication of Amazonas Baptist Hospital.

Victims of a crocodile attack.

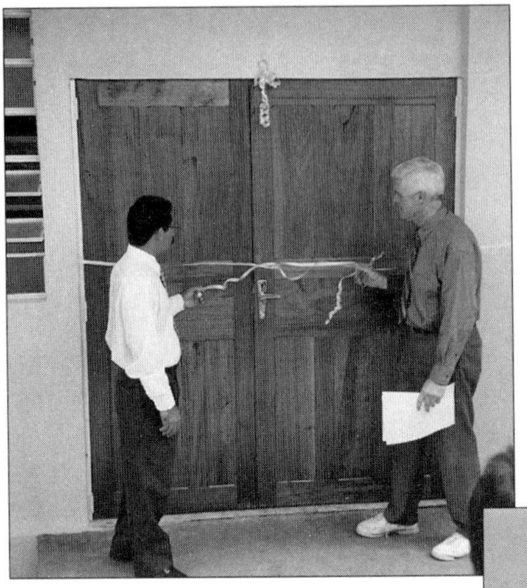

Above:
The mayor of Santo Antônio do Içá and Jack Sorg at the hospital expansion dedication.

Right:
Launch on Amazon River.

Typical housing along Amazon River.

Construction for World Evangelism (CWE) work teams building the hospital addition.

Cessna float plane initially used on the Amazon by Hank Scheltema, later flown by his son-in-law, Al Yoder.

Local people playing native instruments.

Thatched-roof housing in Santo Antônio do Içá, Brazil.

Above:
Construction begins on the hospital addition, 1997.

Left:
Completed addition to the Amazonas Baptist Hospital, 1998.

Tropical fruits in the wild.

Amazon River rainforest between Tabatinga and Santa Antônio do Içá, Brazil.

Brazilian mother and daughter.

Missionary pilot Al Yoder in his office.

MYTH NO. 7

Brazilians Don't Want Us There

"We shouldn't let those foreigners in."

Jack and Sandy Sorg began medical evangelism in Santo Antônio do Içá before the hospital was built. During the years of construction, they used an old clinic building owned by the city. They also made house calls, at which Sandy was often the midwife for normal deliveries, calling Jack only when she had a problem.

Four Case Studies

Wedding After Nine Children: Pepito and Florinda, with their eight children, lived in a small, two-room house. The house had walls on three sides, and Pepito slowly earned enough money to enclose the remaining side. Sandy's main difficulty as midwife was providing a little privacy for the mother. Privacy may shrink down to a mosquito net over the bed. All the children were herded into the next room, but peered through the simple open doorway to hear the little one's first cry. Sandy struggled with the placenta while shooing children and curious neighbors away.

Two months later Pepito and Florinda asked the Sorgs to be witnesses at their marriage! As Christians they had become convicted that their 12-year "arrangement" needed to be formalized. All the children came to the simple ceremony in their best clothes. The youngest Sorg daughter, Suzanne, had received a new doll for Christmas and used the clothes for the newborn baby.

Delivery on the Verandah: On another occasion, Sandy passed the clinic building and noticed a young woman, with a pained look on her face, sitting in one corner of the verandah. She was waiting for the morning clinic to open and hoping that her baby wouldn't arrive before then. Her first baby had been slow in coming, so she reasoned this one would also.

As Sandy stepped on the porch, the woman's labor pains increased. Sandy helped the woman lie down and discovered the baby was arriving at that very moment. Some of the other staff arrived in time to bring clean clothes and an instrument to cut the umbilical cord. Other staff members kept the arriving morning clinic patients out in the road until the verandah was free. Sandy slept well that night.

Gloriete was a pretty young mother who worked at the telephone company. Sandy had delivered one of her three children and, with Jack, had taken care of the others when they came to the clinic. A relationship began to grow, creating opportunity for Sandy to talk with her about trusting Christ. For several weeks Gloriete attended the Sunday night services at Faith Baptist Church.

Jack was preaching one night and the Holy Spirit was again working in Gloriete's heart. The severe family resistance to her becoming a Christian, which she was encountering, hindered her, but at the invitation that night, she responded. Sandy prayed with her as Gloriete asked the Lord Jesus Christ to be her Savior.

Penicillin at the Wake: On another occasion, Jack returned to a Santo Antônio house where a young child had pneumonia. The witch doctor had treated the child for days, but when he saw the child was close to death, he sent the boy to Dr. Sorg. This referral was not out of concern for the child, but due to the local superstitions about responsibility. Spiritists teach that the last person to touch a person before he dies is responsible for that death.

The witch doctor knew the child was dying. He also knew that Dr. Sorg would touch the child in the course of the examination, so the blame would be shifted to the American. Jack was used to this, understood the thinking, and tried to teach about germs, infection, and not delaying in seeing the doctor.

Medicine had been in short supply for weeks. Jack had long-acting penicillin, which is useful for a strep throat but not for severe pneumonia. Nevertheless, it was all he had. To space out the painful injections, Jack gave one the first morning he saw the child, and returned shortly after lunch to see how the boy was doing.

He found the family gathered around a small table where the body of the dead child lay. The crowded room was lit by a dozen candles around the body to "light the way of his soul into heaven." Since most of the villagers' beliefs combined spiritism and Roman Catholic Church teaching, the priest had been called. He was leaving as Dr. Jack arrived.

Jack paid his respects to the grieving family, and noticed many family members were coughing. The dead boy had had a cough for a number of days before dying. During the wake, Jack circulated with his stethoscope. At the invitation of all the guests, he listened to the respiration of the people present. No one had pneumonia, but the coughs of several revealed severe bronchitis.

Worried parents pleaded with Jack to inject the medicine he had brought for the child into the rest of the coughing family members. So during the wake, Jack went from person to person, adults and children, giving penicillin injections.

This type of love shown to the people of Brazil has resulted in a respect for the hospital. Today, the Amazonas Baptist Hospital has solid credibility for hundreds of miles up and down the river. Because of the services of the hospital, missionary presence and the preaching of God's Word have gone from being tolerated to being accepted. But that was not always the case. Protective of their turf, a few people opposed the hospital before and during construction. Some of the earliest and harshest criticism came from a Roman Catholic priest.

Some Roman Catholic priests are ecumenical, some are neutral, and others actively dislike Protestants. One of the two priests in Santo Antônio do Içá was in the latter camp and wanted neither Bible-believing missionaries nor a Baptist hospital in town.

As the Sorgs prepared for their 1983 move to Santo Antônio do Içá, the priest appeared before the city council to argue against hospital construction. He is reported to have said, "We shouldn't allow these foreigners into our city!" A believer on the council reminded the priest that he himself was a foreigner from Italy. The priest's objection voiced to the city council was the opening salvo of the struggle missionaries would have with this man for the next several years.

Life Saving Rescues Child and Clinic: The city council gave permission for the hospital to be built. In spite of that victory, trouble still brewed. On one of Dr. Sorg's visits to the small clinic in Santo Antônio do Içá, he was asked to see an infant. The little boy needed a minor medical procedure. A few drops of Novocaine® were injected at the incision site, and the baby stopped breathing!

Dr. Sorg had little in the way of supplies. All the medicines on hand would have fit in a shoe box: no oxygen masks or bags to help the child breathe, no suction machines to clean out secretions, no medicines to help stimulate the child. Dr. Sorg reported:

"I began mouth-to-mouth resuscitation, working for almost two hours until the medicine reaction began to wear off, and the child began spontaneous respiration. During these two hours, we found some old IV tubing, cut it off and, aspirating on the end like a straw, we were able to suction out the child's secretions. Then a woman helped me find epinephrine nose drops (similar to adrenaline). We put a few drops in his nose and mouth to speed up his low heart rate. I was totally absorbed in maintaining this child with mouth-to-mouth, trying not to breathe too hard (which would blow out his lungs), trying not to breathe too fast (which would slow the restarting of his respiration), but trying to breathe fast enough to give him good color in his skin (which means he is getting enough oxygen).

"Meanwhile, two things were happening outside. The Roman Catholic priest, who was opposed to our being in town, was running door-to-door, telling everyone that I was killing a child. Not much goes on in town, so the story spread quickly and a crowd of about 200 local citizens gathered outside the clinic. I didn't know the crowd was gathering, nor why, nor that my reputation was on the line.

"The other occurrence was at the hospital construction site. Most of the workers were believers in Christ. Knowing what was happening, they interrupted construction and started a prayer meeting for me.

"After two hours, the child started breathing on his own with good color. Another two hours and he was ready to go home. Completely exhausted, I emerged from the clinic along with the baby and his mother. There stood the 200 silent watchers, awaiting word. The mother smiled, showed off the child, and gave me high marks for saving his life. I closed the clinic for the rest of the afternoon, went home, and fell into bed."

The hospital is well established in Santo Antônio, but has less impact on the Indians who live in remote areas. Some Indians don't like to come to the hospital because they are afraid no one will be able to translate for them. Others don't come because they fear the doctor will want to keep them in the hospital instead of sending them away with just a shot. Few come from Betânia, a large Indian community of about 1,500, just 20 miles away from the hospital. By contrast, Jui, a non-Indian Brazilian town, is five times farther away, but has five times as many patients at the hospital. A few Indians, even Christian Indians, may not come because they depend on witch doctors, a hard influence to break.

Serving the people of the Amazon is complicated by the fact

that many patients are brought to the hospital after several weeks or months of either self-treatment or witch-doctoring. Some are incapable of assisting with the diagnosis:

Dr. Jack: "When did you first notice the pain?"

Answer: "The day Aunt Sue came to visit, maybe it was a week after the big tree fell in the yard."

Dr. Jack: "Does it hurt worse on the right side, or the left?"

Answer: "Yes."

Dr. Jack: "How long has the coffee bean been up this infant's nose?"

Answer: "Three or four months."

Dr. Jack: "Why did you wait so long to come to the hospital?"

Answer: "We thought it would fall out sooner or later."

It's true, some people on the Amazon don't want ABWE's hospital there, but the other 99% do!

Practicing medicine from the government clinic convinced us we needed a hospital. Naively, we thought the hospital would be up and running within a short time.

MYTH NO. 8

It Won't Take Long to Build a Hospital Here

"American Christians will come to help, so missionaries won't be much involved in the building effort."

With the money in hand and personnel on the horizon, Jack Sorg set out to build a hospital along the Amazon River.

Building the Hospital

Brick, rock, wood, cement, and steel: each was a trial to accumulate. The height of the Amazon River varies as much as 30 feet during the year (April–May is the highest water time; October–November the lowest.) At low water, deltas can be harvested for *sand*. Local people were paid 15 cents for a five-gallon bucket of sand.

Bricks, not available locally, were purchased from a factory 40 miles away. Transportation costs doubled the price, since each brick was handled many times before arrival in Santo Antônio.

Getting *rocks* to mix in the concrete added a new experience for local people: the rock test. There is almost no rock in the area. But at low water, rocks can be found about a mile away. People loaded their boats and canoes to the safety point, bringing rock to the center of town for Dr. Sorg's rock test. If the rocks crumbled when he smashed them together, they were no good. But if the rocks broke into several pieces with a "clink," they were hard enough to use.

The hospital is constructed of brick and cement, with only doors and window screen frames made of wood. But a large amount of *wood* was needed for the forms into which the concrete was poured. You might think, *No problem. We were building in one of the greatest forests in the world!* Right? Wrong. The wood came from a distant mill, rough-cut in non-uniform widths and lengths. A 1 in. x 8 in. came in widths 6 in. to 12 in. wide, 3/4 in. to 1-1/2 in. thick, varying in length from 8 to 12 feet. With a board planer from the States, crews created uniform lumber for forms.

Cement could only be purchased in the city of Manaus, 750 miles away. Burly Brazilians loaded the ferry in Manaus and off-loaded it in Santo Antônio do Içá.

Steel girders for the roof section were each over 30 feet long. Tied on top of the old VW van, they hung ten feet over the front and back of the van. Navigating slowly through the narrow streets was tricky.

That old van literally transported the hospital to the site, piece by piece. It gave up its life for the hospital, totally trashed by the time construction was completed. The van was the workhorse for hauling sand, rock, bricks, cement, wood, steel, and most of the supplies. For a long time, it was the only operational vehicle in town. The roof caved in, and the inside wore out, but the VW van lasted through the construction.

People-Building that Builds People

Constructing the hospital took three years. Delays in getting materials, the slow trickle of additional donations, and worker inexperience hindered progress. All the fixtures, tile, doors, windows, electrical and sanitation tubing, and wiring had to be purchased in Manaus. Sometimes the construction crew forged ahead, making good progress, until a missing item ground work to a halt. The first step to get the needed item was an "iffy" phone call to Manaus. The hope was that the material would arrive within about ten days on the local river "taxi" boat. And somebody had to meet each one.

Worker inexperience contributed to the long construction time. One day, Jack marked an "X" near a line where he wanted a wall built. Returning to check on progress, he discovered the wall had been built on the wrong side of the line, missing the foundation beneath. The wall had to be torn down. Laborers unfamiliar with design in tile installed it without regard to pattern.

The Brazilian foreman showed workers how to do the first part of an electrical or plumbing job, then returned to correct mistakes as the work progressed. Then he instructed them in the next phase. All this took a long time, and when the hospital was finished everyone felt a great sense of accomplishment. "We ended up with a local church that was trained in masonry, carpentry, and other skills," said Jack.

At the time of construction, the Baptist church members were among the poorest in town. The monthly offering in church was rarely more than $5. Due to politics, Christians were not given opportunities for good jobs. When the Sorgs arrived, only two men in the church had jobs which paid them monthly salaries.

To help raise their economic status, Dr. Sorg hired believers to build the hospital. Part of the stipulation for hiring them was that they had to attend church faithfully and tithe. Suddenly the church began to enjoy a healthy budget. Today, some of the church members are still able to make a living using the skills they learned during the construction phase of the hospital.

By the end of the hospital construction, Faith Baptist Church in Santo Antônio do Içá had a building fund sufficient to build a new church twice the size of the old one, and experienced masonry workers to build it.

While the hospital construction was going on, Carolynn Sharp conducted a training program for nurses. The goal was that trained nursing attendants would be ready by the time the hospital opened its doors.

Hospital Expansion

Building that first hospital took three years, a long period over which to sustain determination, drive, and energy while carrying out regular responsibilities. The extent of Jack's construction knowledge at that time was expanding his rental house in Manaus using a *Better Homes & Gardens* construction book. Jack Sorg and the national believers did a marvelous job!

By 1990, however, the medical team had outgrown the eight-bed facility. Expansion was necessary, but Jack knew he couldn't oversee construction this time. On furlough ministries in 1991, while preaching in Tampa, Florida, Jack was introduced to Paul Puleo. This man had recently started a missionary-helps agency known as Construction for Worldwide Evangelism (CWE). This organization, based in Tampa, Florida, exists to assist missionaries with their building projects.

Paul Puleo, the CEO at Construction for Worldwide Evangelism, was reluctant to accept responsibility for construction of such a remote facility, not certain he could ensure a quality building. With resupply 750 miles away in Manaus, CWE looked carefully at this job. A small team came to Santo Antônio in 1993 to construct Sunday school classrooms. This smaller pilot project served as an experiment to see if constructing a larger hospital was possible.

In the spring of 1996, CWE formally committed to the huge task of doubling the square footage of the Amazonas Baptist Hospital.

CWE sought 100 North American volunteers to go to the site and build the expansion. Over 13 months, five different teams went to the hospital. Each team of 20 workers had men and women, some skilled and some unskilled. The masonry, electrical, plumbing, and painting aspects of the construction all needed to be orchestrated in sequence. Each trip needed skilled tradesmen to direct laborers. Each team went to Santo Antônio do Içá for 12 days of building.

Paul Puleo and his organization assumed responsibility for the integrity of the building. The headaches of supply, standards, drawings, employment for locals, and many, many details would be on Paul's shoulders. "Actually," director Paul Puleo says, "we are building people; secondarily we build buildings."

Teams came from Georgia, the Carolinas, Michigan, and Iowa. What a beautiful spirit was seen in these workers who came at their own expense to expand the hospital.

In between the construction teams' trips, much finishing work was done by local people under the supervision of ABWE missionary Brian Williams.

Construction time for the hospital expansion was not three years. Within 13 months it was dedicated. And Jack Sorg didn't have to become a construction boss. This time, he didn't have to run a clinic at a separate location half the day and then invest the other half of his day supervising construction. Another ABWE doctor, however, *was* involved in the construction project. Dr. Mark Thompson wrote the following story for the summer 1998 issue of the *Message* magazine.

Dedication of Life and Property

"As we pulled up to the port of Santo Antônio do Içá, Donna and I eagerly scanned the crowds to see if we recognized any faces. Four years ago, we left Brazil as short-term missionaries and now we were returning for a two-week construction trip.

"A few weeks earlier we met Bruce and Karleen Johnson of Construction for Worldwide Evangelism, which was responsible for the expansion of the Amazonas hospital.

"Learning of two cancellations on the construction team, Donna and I decided to go. We had only three weeks to get visas, pack our bags with donated hospital supplies and Portuguese Bibles, and drive to Florida to leave our children with my parents.

"Much needed to be completed before the February 14, 1998,

dedication. For 10 days men worked long hours hanging doors, wiring outlets and lights, painting the building, and constructing a 10,000-gallon water tank. Women cooked, cleaned, and laundered. I spent most mornings in surgery with Dr. Jack Sorg.

"The morning of the dedication, I swept the floor and carried out trash, praising God for the hundreds of people saved in the past 12 years through medical evangelism. I also praised Him for the beautiful building He provided through the efforts of over 100 CWE volunteers.

"By 9 a.m., hundreds had gathered on the front lawn of the Amazonas Baptist Hospital to witness the dedication. Pastors and local church members praised God. After a final prayer came the grand tour of the hospital's new wing. As we said our farewells at the hospital, Donna and I promised to return as soon as possible.

"Missions was heavily emphasized at Montrose Baptist Church where I grew up. I have many memories of missionary slide presentations and curios from foreign lands. I also enjoyed reading missionary stories and dreamed of being a missionary pilot until I realized I cannot even look down in a car without getting sick. But I still wanted to be a missionary, and eventually my interests turned to medicine.

"When my sisters Mary Ann and Christine became medical missionaries, I experienced missions firsthand. In Togo, West Africa, I did research on river blindness, helped with the construction of the Karolyn Kempton Memorial Christian Hospital, and helped run the lab two different times.

"While in medical school, I visited the Amazonas Baptist Hospital where Mary Ann worked. During family practice training, I debated between going to Togo or to Amazonas for practical experience. Mary Ann wrote about a half-price airline special to Brazil. That's hard for any missionary to turn down! She also wrote about a nurse who impressed her more than any other short-termer. I booked a flight for Brazil, and now I will let that short-termer tell the rest of the story."

Donna, the short-termer, said, "Unlike Mark, missions was not in my plans even though I was saved at an early age. During youth retreats and summer camps I told God I was willing to do whatever He wanted, tacking on *even if you want me to be a missionary.* After completing my schooling, I became the nurse at the Shepherd's Home in Union Grove, Wisconsin. Following two short-term missions trips, I changed my prayer to, *Please, Lord, let it be missions for my life.* Contacting ABWE I accepted the opportunity to work at the Amazonas Baptist Hospital for a year. That was when Mark came to visit."

Donna and Mark were married in 1995, attended Candidate Seminar in 1996, and in February 1999 arrived in Brazil eager to serve the Lord in medical evangelism.

Between February 1997 and February 1998, the hospital building was expanded from an eight-bed facility to a hospital that accommodates 22 inpatients with separate men's, women's, and pediatric wards; an ICU; a labor room; and a large sterilizing/central supply room.

God's people were happy with their church and the hospital. But isn't the Amazon just a sleepy spiritual backwater? Is God doing anything on the Amazon?

MYTH NO. 9

God Isn't Doing Much on the Amazon

"The Amazon's just a sleepy backwater—
nothing happens here."

While the town of Santo Antônio do Içá isn't the new Jerusalem, God is doing something special there. He loves the people of the Amazon region, and He has sent believers there to display His character.

This chapter reports two of those special events: how God got the payroll delivered to workers as the hospital was being constructed, and His long-term working in Betânia, the village composed largely of Ticuna Indian believers.

God and the Payroll Run

Armed only with his experience from expanding his Manaus house and a *Better Homes & Gardens* home improvement book, Dr. Jack Sorg led the hospital construction work beginning in 1983. He spent one-half of his workday at the city clinic, and the other half at the construction site.

Supplies were difficult to get since the hospital is 750 miles away from the city of Manaus, the source of supplies. No volunteers from North America helped with the first phase of construction, but God supplied a capable Brazilian foreman named Moisés. Jack and Sandy met Moisés in Manaus while in language study.

Jack approached him with the challenge to help build the hospital. The timing was right, since Moisés was just finishing a job at a public school in Manaus. The fact that his wife had been raised in Santo Antônio do Içá was another drawing card. Moisés and his family moved to the hospital site just two months after the Sorgs, and the children of both families became close friends.

With no building codes to follow and no inspectors to advise, Jack and Moisés were on their own. Jack went with the theory that if *Good Housekeeping* said to make the wall 20cm thick, he would double it. That was specially true for the foundation. "Everything else we can repair later if we have to," Jack said, "but we can't repair a bad foundation."

Getting money to the site to pay the Brazilian construction workers proved that God is concerned about missions on the Amazon. Money for the payroll came through a U.S. checking account for the field council. The checkbook stayed with the missionaries in Manaus, the location of the money exchange houses. American checks were changed into Brazilian currency, the cash taken upriver 750 miles to the hospital by a roundabout route.

As construction proceeded, Dr. Sorg anticipated payroll needs about two weeks in advance. Telephoning ABWE missionaries in Manaus set the money machine in motion. Normally Jack requested $2,000. While Manaus missionaries had a new telephone and could hear well, the old radio phone in Santo Antônio do Içá had poor reception. So when ABWE missionary Mark Baker in Manaus shouted, Jack could barely hear a "yes" or a "no," and then only if the room was completely quiet.

To beat their low-tech phone equipment, the two men decided that if Mark couldn't hear Jack, Mark would hang up, since Jack could sense a dead line. As long as the line was open, Jack reported on construction progress and needed payroll. Periodically, Jack would ask, "Can you still hear me?" In the distance, Jack could hear a faint "Yes." Yet in Manaus, Mark was yelling "yes" so loudly, the neighbors thought he was fighting with his wife!

In Manaus, Mark would change U.S. $2,000 into Brazilian currency in small bills, usually the only type available. Returning to the bank used for mission business, Mark typically deposited the money in the account of ABWE missionary pilot Clif Jensen, who lived in the town of Benjamin Constant, 1,000 miles upriver from Manaus, and 250 miles west of the construction site. Mark called Clif to inform him that money had been deposited. Benjamin Constant was a small town, so coming up with $2,000 was apt to take a day or two. Clif had to wait until the bank notified him that enough people had deposited money so that he could withdraw $2,000.

Payroll money in hand, Clif bought vegetables or something needed in Santo Antônio do Içá. He then proceeded to the waterfront and hid the "lettuce" among the vegetables in the box. The local ferry boats took the box, sitting out on an open deck, through frequent stops and with hundreds of people coming and going.

The next challenge was getting word to Jack that the money was on its way. Because of bureaucratic red tape, a radio license was unobtainable, so there was no direct link between Clif and Jack. Clif radioed John Kallin in Foz do Jutaí. That communication link leaped eastward over the hospital site by 125 miles because John lived that far downriver from the hospital.

Using his private radio, John Kallin reached Lindsey Harrell in Betânia, 15 miles upriver, west of the hospital. Lindsey wrote a note and dispatched an Indian to paddle the 15 miles to the hospital site.

This process was so drawn out that the boat sometimes arrived the same day Dr. Sorg received his note. Sometimes the boat arrived the very hour the note did. On other occasions, the box was left on the dock, and the note arrived afterwards. A missionary would rush to the waterfront to find the box sitting along the road with the hospital's name on it. After a day in the Amazon heat, the vegetables weren't fresh, so everyone left the smelly box alone! At other times, Brazilian friends pulled the box out of the sun and held it for the hospital. Sometimes the boat people just gave the box to someone and trusted him to deliver it. One time Jack got a note from a passer-by, "I have a little box here in town whenever you want it."

On another occasion, coming late to the waterfront, Dr. Sorg frantically asked about the expected box. People at the waterfront said, "The boat owners had a box for you, but since no one came for it, they decided to save it for delivery on their next trip." Biking back to the house, the doctor hopped in his speedboat. After pursuing the ferry for ten miles, he drew alongside. Dr. Sorg said, "The people on board knew what I wanted and just threw the box over the side into my speedboat. I waved a big thanks, checked the box for both kinds of green stuff, and headed back to the hospital."

Dr. Sorg cautiously held the money for two days, lest anyone make the connection with the newly arrived box from Benjamin Constant. This method worked for 15 deliveries over a two-year period totaling $25,000 without any loss. Human error could have broken the chain at any number of places. The Lord protected even the payroll for the progress of His work on the Amazon.

Betânia

The Ticuna Indians are the largest tribe in South America. Around 50,000 are scattered throughout Brazil, Peru, and Colombia; 30,000 live in Brazil. ABWE's work among these people is a wonder-filled story.

In the late 1940's, indigenous Ticunas, scattered along the Içá, Solimões, and Pana rivers, heard that a man in Santo Antônio was talking about God. They looked for him when they took their produce to town. "We saw Andres using his old record player, telling people about God," said Maria Flores, sister of the future pastor in Betânia. Though fearful of this strange white man, Maria accepted a Bible. "I read a little from the Bible and then our family traveled back home. I told my family about the man who had the Word of God and talked to us about God." The Indians started to tell others about this man and what he was telling them.

Maria continues, "In 1952, my family moved into Santo Antônio do Içá. We kept learning from this missionary. I sang with his three daughters. This went on while I was growing up. When I was 15 years old, the family returned to their native Scotland to retire. In 1960, other missionaries came and taught the same thing. Their names were Lindsey (locally known as Eduardo) and Jean Harrell. I helped the missionaries with music and taught local people to read."

Dale and Martha Payne began work with the Brazilian people in Santo Antônio do Içá in 1966, while the Harrells continued to focus on the Ticuna Indians. Both missionary families lived in Santo Antônio. They envisioned a multi-cultural church made up of both Brazilian and Ticuna believers.

But the Ticuna believers experienced problems with some of the non-Christian Brazilians. On the edge of town near the Harrells, the Ticunas cleared large areas for farming. Problems began when the townspeople's cows ate the Indians' crops. A Ticuna tells what happened next: "An Indian put a hole in one of their bulls, and many of the Indians were thrown into jail."

The Indians' hard work in clearing the land made the plots attractive, and Brazilians, *civilizados*, wanted the land. These "civilized" people registered the Indians' land in their own names, and muscled out the Indians.

In addition to conflicts with non-Christians, cultural differences with the Brazilian believers over such things as language, beliefs, and family structure proved too great for the Harrells and the Paynes to plant a combined Ticuna–Brazilian church. The Ticunas chose to move away and establish their own community and church.

Loving the Indian people, Lindsey Harrell set out to help them. He found a tract of land 15 miles up the Içá River. For a ridiculously few hundred dollars, he bought Betânia, a parcel two-thirds of a mile by three miles, located on Lake Caruara. He registered it in the name of the mission, so it was safe from encroachment, but gave the land to the Ticunas.

The Harrells built a home at Betânia and settled in to disciple the Indian believers in their faith, and to enhance the quality of their lives. For the next 16 years, Lindsay and Jean poured themselves into the Ticunas. As living sacrifices, they rendered service in which North American Christians would be proud to have invested. Over 2,900 Indians live in Betânia today; 900 of whom belong to the Betânia Baptist Church.

Eventually all the Ticunas from Santo Antônio moved to this land, which became the town of Betânia. The Harrells started a school and taught the Bible. Now most Betânians can read and write. When the Evangelical Regular Baptist Church of Betânia was started, a nine-year-old boy named Jordão Flores was saved and committed his life to the Lord Jesus Christ. Growing in the Lord, he is now the co-pastor of the church.

Speaking of the work in Betânia, Pastor Jordão Flores said in 1996, "The Word of God was preached by Lindsey Harrell and our Ticuna preacher, Pastor Modestino. Many came to know Christ as Savior. The village grew to over 2,000 people. The Lord has kept His work growing. God is doing an important work here. The believers are strong spiritually. Each day, I see people seeking His will. They are consecrating their lives to God. Though each generation questions their parent's faith, we are seeing progress among the young people."

The church leaders have the equivalent of a high school education. Both the Old and New Testaments are available in the Ticuna language, and the pastors study the Word in their native language and in Portuguese.

Pastor Jordão Flores added, "We need missionaries and pastors, American or Brazilian. I don't have enough practical experience to serve the 500 active members of the congregation. We also need more theological education for the younger men, our future leaders."

Grace for Lago Grande

While Betânia was being established, a small group of malcontent Ticunas arose. As Christian values grew to dominate the fledgling village, the atmosphere was not to the liking of the minority. "We want to party and carouse; we don't want to live in Betânia. Your lives are a bore!"

Unwilling to live by the rules established by the Indian believers (no beer, wine, or tobacco sales in town), they looked for a separate location for an independent, free-spirited community.

They chose Lago Grande ("Big Lake"), ten miles from Santo Antônio do Içá, at the mouth of the Içá River. Outsiders attempting to reach Lago Grande were met with machete-armed toughs who gave a clear message: "Stay away." Villagers didn't want visitors who might report their marijuana crops. Even the federal military were met at the shoreline by machete-wielding men, preventing them from getting out of their boats. Returning with more muscle, the military raided the village and arrested the offenders.

In God's grace, relatives from Betânia visited this rebel community and witnessed to family members. The Holy Spirit also worked through the hospital. Sick residents of Lago Grande experienced the loving care of godly medical workers, and heard the "Good News" in the hospital, further softening their attitudes.

Through that nucleus of people whose hearts the Lord had softened, the village allowed staff from the hospital to visit. Gradually, a few people at Lago Grande became believers. The door to Lago Grande cracked open.

Missionaries assisted the Indian believers in building a simple church. Today, this previously resistant, defiant community has a vibrant voice, speaking God's love.

Consider the testimony of Elinaro Morais:

"I am certain that my salvation is in Christ Jesus. Most of the people in this community are now saved. We are praying for those who have not yet accepted Christ, so that we will all become a loving family in Jesus' name.

"Before I was saved, I lived in the world of Satan. I would get drunk and fight. When the missionaries came, I watched them from afar, unwilling to listen. But when I finally decided to listen and opened my heart to Christ, my life changed. Thank the Lord! Today I am saved. He has brought a lot of happiness to us and now we are growing all the time in Christ's love and peace. Many people from the surrounding areas are hearing about Christ and coming to live with us in this community. Our church is growing, and when other people come to visit, there is not enough room. We are hoping we can build a larger church building. Physically we are poor, but spiritually we are rich. We have about three homes in our community where the family members have not accepted Christ, but slowly these families are beginning to listen to us. In one three-month period, 62 people were baptized and we have more who are ready."

God is at work on the Amazon; it's a myth to believe otherwise. But some people are suspicious of technology, seeing science as the god of this age, usurping the omnipotence of God. Is modern day technology unspiritual?

MYTH NO. 10

Technology Is Unspiritual

"Who needs that stuff? Most people still can't operate a computer."

The Amazonas Baptist Hospital admits to owning and using sophisticated technology to assist God's healing of bodies and souls. Three situations serve as examples that God uses modern technology to achieve His purpose.

The Airplane and the Alligator

ABWE missionaries plant churches among both Brazilians and Ticuna Indians along the Amazon borders of Peru, Brazil, and Colombia. In 1976 church-planting pilots Al Yoder and Clif Jensen explored a remote area, hoping to contact Indians near the village of Belém. Local people in that region were heavily involved in a cult called the Cross Movement. Some members of that group carry a Bible in one hand, and a gun in the other.

Al recalls, "As we taxied up to the riverbank to drop off a gift, we noticed a number of men with clubs, stakes, and other war-like tools dotting the beach." *This is not going to be a friendly visit,* Al thought. He tied the plane to a stake, and called to his ten-year-old daughter, Regina, in the cockpit. "Honey, leave the doors locked. Don't open them for anyone, even if they act friendly." At the time, Al had a broken foot—the result of a recent soccer game—so he was not walking well.

Calling to some Indian men who had come to the the river's edge, Al said, "I'm here to talk to the captain (chief of the village). I have something to give him." Hoping for a favorable reception because of the gift, Al moved up the bank as he awaited their response.

Behind him, he heard a loud bang. Turning, he saw the Indians had removed the stake to which the plane was tied, thrown it at the airplane, and pushed the airplane out into the river. Al Yoder continued, "My daughter was inside the airplane being swept away by a strong current. With a bad foot, I couldn't run, so I yelled, 'My baby, my baby!'"

In the providence of God, an Indian believer from one of the downriver churches was visiting in the village. Describing that moment, Al said, "Reacting instantly to my cry, he hit the water like a fish and, with great exertion, brought the airplane back to the bank. Not wanting to stay for tea, I dropped the package, hobbled down to hug my Indian friend, limped into the plane, and flew home. I thought, *I'm not going back there, at least not with my daughter.*"

But God was interested in the people of that village. Just two weeks later, a call came from Belém. "We have a crocodile bite victim. Can you fly down and save this young man?" Expecting no hassles this time, but a bit leery of the sight of what an alligator can do to a human body, Al took off on the medivac run.

Hearing the airplane engine, the Indians carried a body wrapped in a blood-red sheet toward the bank to meet the plane. "As they were stuffing the victim into the plane, someone was jabbering about how the man had been fishing where he should not have been, how he fell in, and how the alligator had torn him up," said Al. "Look," the Indians encouraged, opening the sheet. Bone was visible.

Through good medical care, the young man survived and healed. Who was this young man? None other than the son of the village captain. The grateful captain met the returning flight, gave

Al the red carpet treatment, and said, "Anything you want and any time you want it, it's yours. Come and hold your gospel meetings in our area."

At that time, Al Yoder had such a busy schedule he was not able to open this new preaching point. But he told the Indian pastors and believers about the opportunity. Even though it meant 12 hours of paddling in their canoes, the believers took up the challenge to start a church in Belém. After holding some gospel meetings, however, the believers were ordered not to return. Occasionally, Ticuna Indians visiting relatives invite neighbors in for singing and Bible teaching, but there is no church in Belém yet.

Even so, the natural wrath of an alligator advanced the kingdom of God, and the high-tech airplane played a role.

The Talking Box

Manoel and his family squatted around the transistor radio. Radio transmission from Trans World Radio was normally good between 3 a.m. and 5 a.m. But weak batteries and static reduced reception, making it hard to understand what the box was saying.

Manoel caught a few words: "a gift," "peace," "sin." Manoel knew that he had done bad things: beaten his wife, gotten drunk, and caroused. Always one to appease the gods, Manoel was petrified of the evil spirits. When he went hunting, he hid so that Curupira, the feared demon god of the jungle, wouldn't find him. Manoel scrunched low in fear when the jaguar screeched in the night. But peace? Never could he find peace.

Manoel continued to listen to the radio, then turned to a friend, "What do you think of that man in the box? I feel this terror inside when I think of Curupira. Some people say there is no such thing as the god of the jungle, but our friend Pedro swears there is and says he's seen the footprints. We must find out about this God who loves," Manoel insisted.

Some time later, Manoel and Pedro paddled their canoe all day down to Jutaí, a village over 100 miles downriver from the hospital. Maybe someone in Jutaí would tell them about the God who loved them. God had prepared for the visit of these two men through the work of two ABWE missionary couples, Ed and Dot Blakslee, who worked in Fonte Boa in 1962; and John and Sylvia Kallin, who pioneered the church planting work in Jutaí, beginning in 1974. John was on hand to receive Manoel and Pedro.

John took his Bible and explained verse after verse to the two canoeists. Then he said, "Tying food to a long pole and hoisting it up to appease the spirits will not bring you peace or freedom from guilt. Doing good deeds will not bring you genuine happiness. Even raising an orphaned child, as your wife has done, will not get you to that happy place after you die. There is nothing you can do to get there. But God loves you and has sent His own Son to this hateful, dirty place to die in man's place. Jesus, God's Son, was a perfect man. He never sinned. If you truly believe," continued John, "that Jesus died for you, ask Him to forgive you of all your sin. He will, and He will give you peace."

John Kallin told the rest of their story: "They understood so well that I was amazed. They had heard Christian radio broadcasts over and over, and had already decided to be saved. They came to see me so they could make the decision 'with a person and do it the right way.' When they came to my door in Jutaí, I asked when they had attended meetings at church. Church? 'Never.' They had never even been inside a church. They had heard the gospel over the radio. They found us before we found them."

The men wanted peace and God's love. They prayed, simply asking God to forgive their sins, believing Jesus died for them as the Bible said. Calm came. The terrible knot disappeared from their stomachs.

With joy, they asked John Kallin to visit their village of Airúa. This village is in the jungle, up uncharted streams, interwoven with other nondescript, look-alike streams. Few North Americans can paddle for two or three days like the locals can. For that reason the missionaries were not able to add Airúa to their already full schedules.

Fifteen years passed from the visit of Manoel and Pedro to Jutaí before anyone held a meeting in Airúa. But one day pilot Clif Jensen's plane touched down in Airúa; the whole village turned out, covering the river bank. Having never seen an airplane, little children clung to their parents; a few screamed in fear. What did these men in the big bird want?

Old gray-haired Faustão, Ticuna Indian leader from Betânia, assured the Airúa villagers, "It's Senhor Eduardo (Lindsey Edward Harrell) from Betânia." Clif Jensen had brought this senior missionary to tell the villagers more about God. The two men John had led to the Lord years before were still living for God. Now, Ticuna Indian believers go to Airúa for meetings.

This chain of events was set in motion by a radio and sustained by an airplane. Technology is a tool God can use for His kingdom.

Air in a Bottle

Nazaré's Testimony: Nazaré was born in Santo Antônio. As a teen she knew something about the Bible from living in Manaus with her aunt. While she was finishing her education in Manaus, Nazaré had no interest in the Word of God. She went to church with her aunt and cousins, but never yielded to God.

Pressured by friends at church, Nazaré made a profession of faith just to satisfy them, but she continued being involved in the wrong kinds of parties and dances. This upset her Christian friends. Since she was not saved, Nazaré did not have the power of the Holy Spirit to help her live a Christian life.

When Nazaré became pregnant outside of marriage, she returned to Santo Antônio and was admitted to Amazonas Baptist Hospital to deliver her baby. While there, she watched a video explaining that the only path to God is through Jesus Christ and the blood He shed for us. That video touched Nazaré's heart, especially when the preacher on the video pointed out that any sexual relationship outside of marriage is prostitution in the eyes of God. That point struck Nazaré powerfully. She promised the Lord she would go to church and really find out about Him.

At church, several believers presented the gospel, and this time Nazaré made a firm, public decision. The Redeemer changed so many values and attitudes in her life that old friends thought she was being extreme.

"Don't you miss going to the bars and drinking beer?"

"Not anymore. Those cravings are replaced with a desire to read the Scriptures and be among other Christians."

Moisés' Testimony: Growing up in Santo Antônio, Moisés was raised in a staunch Roman Catholic family, but didn't know what a true believer in Christ was. The Baptist Church ran attractive youth programs, so Moisés decided to visit their church. He went with some friends who knew Christian young people in the church. Pastor Dionardo preached well, and Moisés decided he wanted to stay after the service and learn more. Instead, he and his friends went to a bar and Moisés forgot about it.

One night in a bar, his friends suggested visiting the Baptist church again. Though drunk, Moisés agreed. Pastor Dionardo welcomed the visitors and, aware of his lifestyle, challenged Moisés to attend a Bible study.

After he sobered up, Moisés was embarrassed that he had agreed to study the Bible and managed to avoid Pastor Dionardo for almost a year.

Moisés and Nazaré had been school friends. Seeing the change in her life after her salvation, Moisés began attending church with Nazaré. She urged him to study the Bible with the pastor. Moisés was teaching night classes, and his only free time was between 10 p.m. and midnight. The dedicated pastor met with Moisés every night, Monday through Friday, until Moisés gave his life to the Lord Jesus Christ.

In this small town, the razzing came pretty quickly: "You're just faking this Bible stuff; you really want to get the girl!" At work, people made fun of him. But when significant, lasting changes appeared in his life—no more drinking and swearing—Moisés won their grudging respect. In 1992, he was baptized, and he and Nazaré were married.

Moisés entered the practical nurses' course, and both he and Nazaré worked in the hospital. They faced many difficulties in their marriage because both had strong, independent personalities.

Nazaré and Moisés had a little daughter, but because of childbearing problems, the couple planned to prevent further pregnancies. Then Nazaré became pregnant with twins. They were born prematurely, and the hospital staff knew that none born that small had survived.

"If they make it for ten days, they will most likely live," said Dr. Jack Sorg.

Nazaré stayed in the hospital with her babies, and each morning Moisés rose in fear, walked to the hospital, and enjoyed a flood of relief when he saw the babies fighting for life.

The crisis came when Dr. Sorg noticed the diminishing oxygen level in the tank that was the twins' lifeline. With only a little left, Moisés called other towns for another tank; none was available, or the owners would not loan out a tank. A hospital in São Paulo de Olivência said they could supply oxygen, but the babies would have to be taken there. The parents realized that no other place would care for their babies as well as at Santo Antônio, and decided not to move them.

"By tomorrow, the oxygen will be gone," Jack told them. This scared everyone because whenever the medical staff tried to take the twins off the oxygen, they turned pale and had to be put back on the oxygen.

Suddenly, around 10 o'clock that night, the twins didn't need the oxygen anymore. They have grown up to be healthy children—a triumph of God's grace linked with technology.

After the babies went home from the hospital, Moisés and Nazaré became less consistent in church attendance. Walking the half mile with twin babies, one-year-old Tiago, and five-year-old Timoteo was draining. They missed Pastor Dionardo, who had moved away, and became discouraged by financial difficulties. They were cheated out of the money they had put into a city plan to have a new house built. Satan used these things to cause spiritual coldness, and they drifted from the church. But God was still at work.

Nazaré enjoyed working in the kitchen, baking bread and pastries. One day, she put out a sign saying she would sell breads, sweets, and meals. At first her husband objected because the children created so much work for her, but he agreed to let her try. Right from the start, the bakery business boomed. Other places in town served meals, but people preferred Nazaré's in spite of its lack of tables and chairs. ABWE missionary Beth Peace helped Nazaré become the best cake decorator in town. Moisés and Nazaré realized the popularity of their little bakery was God's provision for them. By 1997 Moisés and Nazaré were once again faithful to the Lord, helping in both church and hospital projects.

The airplane, the radio, the cylinder of oxygen: all part of modern life. Technology is a wonderful thing, but apart from the Spirit of God at work, nothing of spiritual significance can happen. Missionaries preach the gospel, but does everyone respond? All who come to the hospital are given loving care, but do they all become Christians?

MYTH NO. 11

Medical Missionaries Treat Only Physical Needs

"Eight skin grafts aided her recovery. The staff lovingly served her. Surely she would come to faith in Christ."

The Lord Jesus Christ and His disciples combined healing with preaching. That combination—a healthy body and spiritual truth—is powerful. Luke 9:2 says, "And he sent them to preach the kingdom of God, and to heal the sick." Physical healing confirmed the authenticity of the Lord Jesus and spoke eloquently about the One who could also heal the soul. In much the same way—though to a lesser degree—the medical ministry of ABWE seeks to do the same thing.

A Christian's task is to put God's character on display. As God is gracious, so missionary doctors, nurses, and church planters must be. As God is truth, so must these servants speak the truth.

Mission hospitals gain an entrance into nations that would not welcome church planters. A loving nurse creates an opening into a family which would otherwise resist contact with Bible-believing Christians. Truth is planted in the minds of patients one by one. Some respond.

The goal of ABWE medical missions is to evangelize and to start churches. Without churches, new believers are left in a vacuum.

A church creates the environment in which new believers can grow and reproduce themselves in the next generation.

The Amazonas Baptist Hospital, although the smallest of ABWE's hospitals, is still substantial. The original, eight-bed facility was expanded in 1998 to over 20 beds, an X-ray room, a laboratory, and two operating rooms. The hospital cares for over 350 patients per month.

Patients in the hospital receive tracts and hear gospel messages daily. Videos further explain the Christian life. Hospital workers go from bed to bed, sharing the good news of salvation through faith in Jesus Christ. Teams go out each weekend, contacting patients in their own communities and establishing preaching points for the gospel. Following up hospital evangelism is essential. This follow-up work nearly doubles the professions of salvation and forms the nucleus for local churches established by non-medical missionaries who are a crucial part of the team.

By September 1991, the hospital had been serving the area around Santo Antônio for six years. Dr. Sorg was able to report, "We have three new congregations in their own church buildings with about 200 believers, and three new preaching points are under development." These believers were the results of medical evangelism as the following accounts show.

Dona Basilda: Many patients are treated at the hospital when "local medicine" has failed. Dona Basilda was only 24 years old and eight of her nine children had died. She had already labored for a day and a half in this pregnancy when Dr. Sorg was asked to visit her home. Kneeling on the bamboo floor, he checked her for vital signs and started an IV on the pale, weak woman.

Dr. Sorg described the situation: "She stopped breathing several times. Each time, we revived her. The medical team poured in diligent, continuous care, and a live baby boy was finally born."

Since the village's ancient midwife was present, the staff had to exercise considerable diplomacy. She insisted Dona Basilda drink tea and use poultices of local herbs, some of which were harmless;

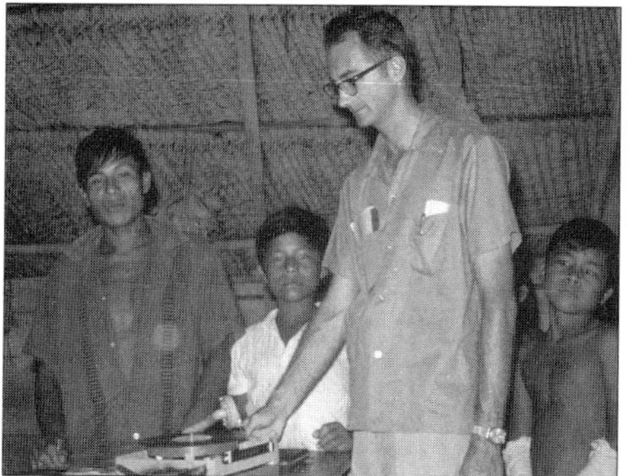

John Kallin preaching in a village.

THE STORY OF ABWE'S MEDICAL WORK
ON THE AMAZON

JUNGLE MYTHS

The van that gave its life for the construction of Amazonas Baptist Hospital.

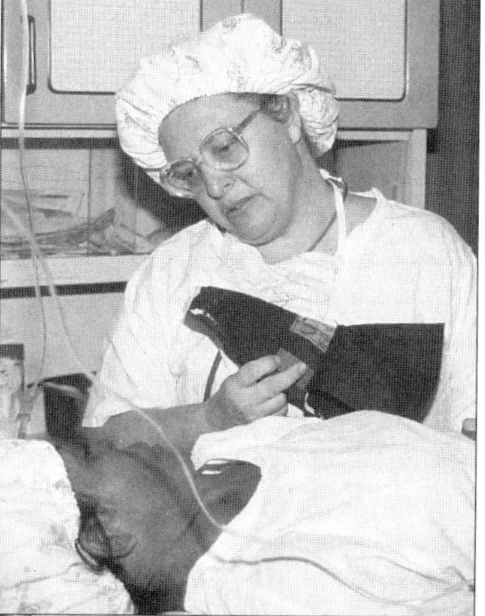

Sandy Sorg, working with a post-op patient.

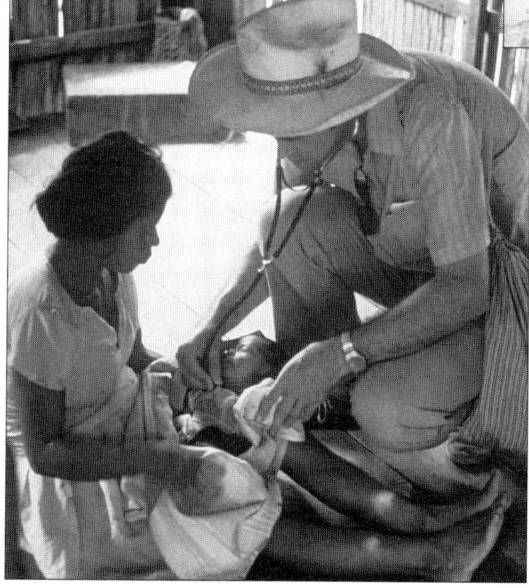

Jack Sorg making a house call.

Lois Wantoch extracting teeth.

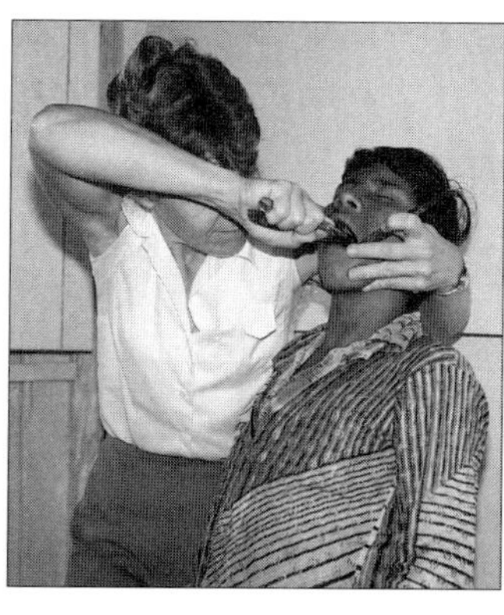

Lindsey & Jean Harrell and family.

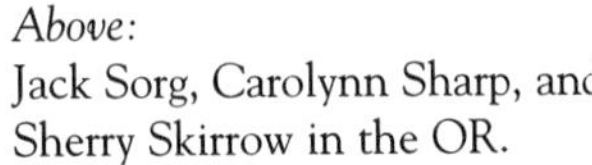

Above:
Jack Sorg, Carolynn Sharp, and Sherry Skirrow in the OR.

Left:
Lois Wantoch teaching Sunday school.

Patty and Bill Hawley, with their youngest son.

Original hospital construction. Pouring cement into forms.

Hospital nurse Ide, daughter of Dona Sofia (first convert from medical work).

Above:
A former patient.

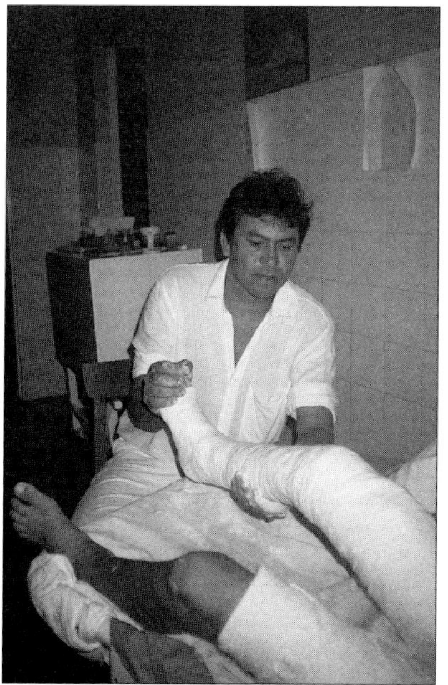

Left:
Hospital employee fitting cast on a patient.

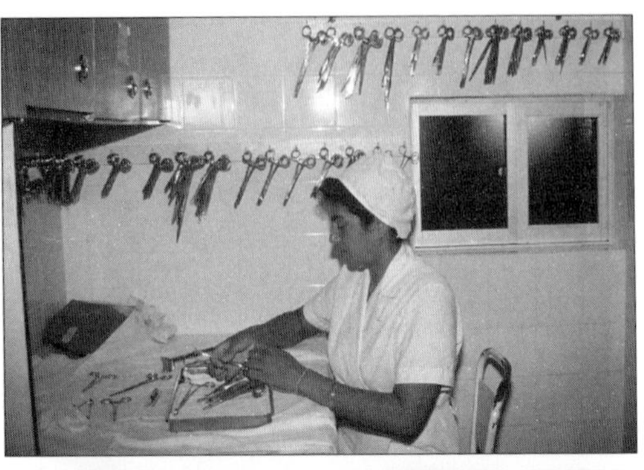
Sterilization department under the care of a faithful Christian woman from the local church.

Jungle home with side kitchen.

Church in Betânia.

Ticuna Indian children.

others were downright dangerous to the baby.

"Crisis begat crisis," wrote Dr. Sorg," as we sought to protect the young mother from local superstitions." Because of the midwife's unsanitary procedures, local medicine, and blood loss, infection set in. Dona Basilda's survival seemed unlikely.

God stepped in with help from an unexpected source, as Dr. Sorg reports. "A passing government boat had IV fluid and antibiotics they were willing to give us. With this help, Dona Basilda began to respond to treatment."

But she needed ongoing care. Reluctantly, the family carried her up the steep, muddy hill to the old government clinic across from the Sorgs' house. This was the facility used for patient care before the hospital building was finished. Hurrying over to check on the mother, nurse Sandy Sorg discovered the newborn had been wrapped in a rag and left back on the floor of the family's hut. An older sister agreed to return home and bring the baby back. Sandy washed him and put him in a laundry basket. During Dona Basilda's slow recovery, the missionaries shared the gospel with her and her family. The baby never grew normally, and Jack diagnosed a cardiac abnormality. The family, the poorest of the poor, couldn't consider seeking medical care in Manaus.

Nurse Carolynn Sharp picks up the story. "We became friends, and I visited Dona Basilda often, sharing the gospel with her. How well I remember the day her baby died. I was at the Sorgs' house when I heard someone running and calling out. From the window I saw Basilda and ran to meet her. I threw my arms around her as she sobbed her heart out and cried, 'My baby died in my arms. While he was crying he just stopped breathing.' The baby was nine months old. Sandy Sorg made a little burial gown for him out of one of her pillow cases.

"We helped her as best we could through that difficult time. A short while later she became pregnant again, and we knew she was at risk for this delivery. Unfortunately, when the time came, Dr. Jack was away, and I was alone in the clinic. When she went into labor I was called to her house urgently, but en route I kept thinking, *I know hardly anything about obstetrics!*

"By the time I arrived, Basilda had delivered her baby boy, Ademar, completely alone. By God's grace, he spontaneously started to cry. Her sister-in-law, Alzira, a believer in Christ, arrived and took the baby. Others of the family started arriving. When I arrived I saw an incredible amount of blood and a roomful of panicky relatives. Basilda was nearly in shock and continued to bleed. As in the previous pregnancy, she again had a retained placenta. I sent someone running for a stretcher which I thought would never arrive! The state health post, which we were using until our hospital opened, was only five or six blocks away. Getting there, however, involved a difficult path, a foot bridge, and an uphill street. 'Oh, Lord,' I prayed, 'Please bring the boat soon. We need Jack, I don't know how to handle this.'

"After putting Basilda in a cot at the clinic, I sent someone to wait at the port for the arrival of the river boat, and to direct Dr. Jack to come immediately to the clinic. Basilda's blood pressure was dropping. We waited and prayed. Soon we heard noise in the street. The doctor was here! Quickly putting on a sterile glove, he performed the required procedure. Basilda's life was spared, and she soon went home where Alzira cared for her. Gradually, with the help of iron supplements, she got stronger.

"At a post-natal check up, Dr. Jack plainly explained the gospel. A few weeks later Basilda attended a Sunday morning service at Faith Baptist Church, and again heard the gospel. Two months after her difficult delivery, Basilda attended church at night, bringing her husband. At the invitation, she and her husband, José, went forward to trust Christ as personal Savior."

This family has struggled in great poverty over the years, with considerable ups and downs spiritually and financially. Dona Basilda cannot read, which makes her spiritual growth more difficult.

The family lives about five miles away from Santo Antônio by canoe, across the Amazon River. Because they could not support themselves in town, they moved to the jungle where the cost of living is cheap, and where hunting and fishing can sustain the family. Dona Basilda comes to church whenever she is in town. Ever grateful for her life being saved, Dona Basilda drops by to visit and to bring some bananas to her missionary friends.

Raimundo: The young man's leg looked bad. The flesh on the inside of the tibia (shin bone) had rotted because of snake venom. The poison hollowed out a cavity about one inch deep, one inch wide, and four inches long. The doctor gently removed the gauze and rebandaged it.

"Just cut off the leg," the youth pleaded. But the doctor knew that the Brazilian Amazon has a Third World economy. Without two good legs in this laborer's world, a person is reduced to pathetic beggary. The young man needed both legs, so the hospital did what was best for him.

"We can save your leg," Dr. Alonso urged. There was a risk in the doctor's decision, because if the young man's leg worsened, he could blame the hospital. That keeps a missionary praying.

With proper treatment, the muscle slowly shook off the effects of the poison and became healthy. The patient brightened and was grateful to have two legs, but to our knowledge he never made a commitment to Christ.

José: At his farm 25 miles away from the hospital, José was bitten by a poisonous snake. Limping into the hospital, he was given the good care all patients receive, along with daily preaching.

Treated for kidney failure and the snake bite over a six-week period, José recovered. Halfway through his stay at the hospital, he became a believer in the Lord Jesus Christ. Three months later, José came to the hospital again, but this time it was not for himself.

"She's been scalped!" cried the nurse. José's wife, Izaura, had leaned too near the rotating shaft of the boat motor. Suddenly, her hair became entangled, and her whole scalp was ripped off her head.

Drs. Bill Hawley and Jack Sorg were in the middle of a C-section when Izaura arrived in a state of shock. Nurse Carolynn Sharp was called out of the operating room to attend to the emergency and began stabilizing the patient. Then Dr. Hawley broke scrub and started treatment to prepare the scalp for re-attachment onto her head. The minute the operating room was available, the staff brought Izaura in to close the gaping wound.

Dr. Sorg reported, "Nothing in my experience prepared me for what I saw. Dona Izaura had lost all her hair, from her forehead back over her head to the back of her neck, and from ear to ear. A family member handed me the thick mane that had been unwound from the drive shaft."

Treatment posed a running battle with infection. Convinced she would die, Izaura's family wanted her to spend her last days at home and pressed for her release. But nurses Sherry, Beth, and Carolynn knew that removing her from the hospital would increase infection and almost certainly kill her. Trusting in God to make good on their word, the staff gave assurances that Izaura would live if she stayed in the hospital. Feeling publicly committed to her recovery, the staff prayed intensely for Izaura and served her diligently.

Izaura heard the gospel week after week, but said "no" to salvation. Eight skin grafts aided her recovery and, in five weeks, Izaura went home: a tiny clearing on a small waterway.

After returning home, José and Izaura opened their house as a preaching point for the weekend ministry of the hospital. A team went to their place every two or three weeks. Izaura wanted the evangelists to come every week, because she had a great hunger for the Word of God.

After healing from her skin grafts, Izaura experienced further tragedy: her seven-year-old granddaughter was killed in a fire when the candle she was holding for her father so he could see to pour gasoline into a tank caught the fuel on fire.

In the spring of 1990, Bill and Patty Hawley rejoiced in the results of their weekend riverboat outreach. On one occasion, they visited house to house in the village of Tonantins. In almost every dwelling, they met someone who had been treated at the Amazonas Baptist Hospital. A special highlight of the weekend was visiting in Izaura's home. After the singing, testimonies, and preaching, Izaura's grown son trusted Christ as his Savior.

Gradually, others in the village professed Christ as Savior. But growth in the Lord is slow, because almost no one in the village is literate. The only gospel truth the people hear is from the teams going out from the hospital once or twice a month. Neither the missionaries nor the government has been able to start a literacy program in these small villages.

Does the hospital care only for physical needs? No. Do all the patients lovingly cared for at the Amazonas Baptist Hospital become Christians? No, but many do. Do all who accept Christ remain strong in their faith? No. Many who are unable to read the Bible for themselves do not grow in their faith. But some do grow spiritually. Often, it is the nurses, involved with the day-to-day patient care, who show the love of Christ most effectively.

MYTH NO. 12

Nurses Aren't Needed Anymore

"Women in white uniforms are yesterday."

The early light of dawn filled the room. Missionary nurse Sherry Skirrow, from Brantford, Ontario, in Canada, blinked awake before the alarm buzzed. Her parrots were talking to each other. Her alarm clock read 5:56. It was Monday morning, and it had been great not to receive any calls during the night.

Making her way into the kitchen, Sherry was greeted by the warm, humid tropical air. Generally, if the missionaries have air conditioning at all, only the bedrooms are air-conditioned. The idea is that if missionaries can get some relief from the humidity and a good night's sleep, they can handle the day.

Chuck Swindoll was discussing Psalm 91 in the book Sherry was reading. Breakfast and the devotional were chewed at the same time. He wrote about irritations, saying that a pearl is the result of an irritation. Should an irritating grain of sand get inside a clam, the clam secretes fluid that surrounds the irritant. Gradually, the multiple layers of this fluid harden into a pearl. *Imagine something good coming from an irritation*, Sherry thought.

She pondered that. Her current term had been long and sometimes discouraging. As acting hospital director, nursing staff supervisor, Bible study leader, and often the nurse on night calls, Sherry had had her share of irritations. *There hasn't been enough of me to go around,* she thought.

In talking with other missionaries, Sherry came to the conclusion that being understaffed and carrying a substantial load is standard missionary fare. The devotional in Psalm 91 provided strength for the day and set a positive tone of anticipation of God's grace.

After cleaning up, Sherry walked the 400 yards to the hospital. Even early in the day, the sun's heat was intense. She avoided the sleeping dogs and the beetles sunning themselves. A few chickens scurried across the path in front of her, and a little black pig oinked and snorted as it probed the grass with its snout.

God's Call on Her Life

Walking to the hospital, Sherry mused about how she had arrived at the Amazonas Baptist Hospital. Her missionary interest had been fed by a missions-minded pastor and her parents, who hosted missionaries in her home as she was growing up.

For a long time Sherry thought missionaries were extraordinary people. After participating in a Missionary Apprentice Program (MAP) trip in 1981 and living with missionaries, she learned that missionaries were ordinary people. That helped Sherry see that God could use her as a missionary.

Unable to find a job immediately after nurses' training, Sherry was challenged to attend London Baptist Bible College in London, Ontario. After graduation, Sherry applied for an MAP assignment in Togo, West Africa. "I can take you to the mailbox where I mailed the application to ABWE, but God worked through the fact that the application never arrived," Sherry reports.

Papua New Guinea, also was a closed door, so Sherry turned to northeast Brazil for a taste of missions. After that six-week MAP experience, Sherry told her mother, "It's a nice place to visit, but I would not want to be a missionary there." Later Sherry said, "The Lord still had work to do in my heart."

That work came through the personal interest shown to her by ABWE missionaries: nurse Carolynn Sharp, and lab/X-ray technician Sue Thomson. Their letters informed Sherry about the need for missionaries on the Amazon. Carolynn wrote, "If you do not feel led to come yourself, please tell others about our need." That appeal is what God used to draw Sherry Skirrow to full-time service on the Amazon. She arrived in August 1987.

All in a Day's Work

Nearing the hospital, Sherry stopped to look at Beth Peace's morning glories, pink and red vincas, and yellow roses, testimonies to God's creativity and pleasant contrasts to jungle green.

Arriving at the hospital, Sherry found the national nurses, housekeepers, and pharmacy and lab techs gathered for devotions. National believers are vital to the hospital; ABWE missionaries could not run a hospital without them. Cristóvão, the staff evangelist, led the singing. Then he spoke on the importance of honesty with God, with one another, and in their work. They prayed concerning the events of the day, then left for their duties.

The verandah held 15 patients that morning. They listened attentively and respectfully to the 15-minute evangelistic presentation. Sometimes it seems there is little fruit, but victory comes through the faithful delivery of the message and loving medical help. God is responsible to save people. God has promised that He will be at work as His truth is made known. After his message, Cristóvão handed out tracts, which people read as they waited to be seen.

By 7:30, Sherry was in the in-patient ward. She checked charts to be appraised of major problems, and listened as the night nurse gave the patient report:

- A 20-year-old soldier had become dehydrated. Too weak to stand, he was admitted and treated with fluids and parasite medication.
- A woman with a history of cirrhosis, anemia, and hepatitis B

was vomiting blood. On a previous hospital visit she had been saved.

- An 11-year-old girl was on intravenous antibiotics for an abscess deep in her thigh. An attempt at aspiration had proven unsuccessful.
- A pregnant young lady was vomiting because of pyelonephritis.

Dr. Daniel Carrel, a short-term doctor from Grand Rapids, Michigan, was there to care for these patients. If no doctor is at the hospital, medical decisions and treatment fall to the nurses.

"Sherry, a snake bite victim is coming in," a Brazilian nurse called from the doorway.

Groaning, agony showing on his face, the man held his swollen right ankle. Two fang-marked puncture wounds were clearly identified by oozing blood. Sherry started an IV, gave the patient an injection for pain, and began a treatment to neutralize the venom. Dr. Carrel injected a sedative.

Sherry continued the treatment around the wound and up the leg to reduce the chance of gangrene. Previously, the hospital had used anti-venin, but the medicine was good only if the patient got to the hospital quickly. The longer you wait the less effective the anti-venin is.

This man had been on the path to his potato garden at 4 a.m. when he stepped on a large jararaca snake coiled in the path. Aroused, the snake bit the man's ankle. The victim climbed into his canoe and paddled upriver for four hours to get to the hospital. (If the Amazonas Baptist Hospital had not been in Santo Antônio, this man would have had to travel five hours farther for treatment.) Sherry was encouraged by the certainty that the hospital was making a difference in people's lives.

After the staff got the man with the snake bite onto the ward, Sherry started to care for the patients on the verandah. Suture removals, obstetrical checks, wound rechecks. Sherry scheduled some patients for the afternoon. She instructed some patients with abdominal pain, fever, or diarrhea to turn in a stool exam, and those with urinary complaints to give a urine specimen. It was a busy morning, but every little interruption reminded her of the good-sized pearl being formed by the irritations.

Sherry was pleased to see a young man who had returned for his sutures to be removed. Since no doctor had been present when he came in, Sherry had sutured the machete wound on his foot. His wound had healed nicely.

Late in the morning, Sherry ushered a young man in to see the doctor. Five months earlier, he stepped on a piece of glass. Though he dug some of it out himself, he didn't get it all. Periodically, he took an antibiotic because the wound became infected. Sherry set out the I & D set (incision and drainage instruments) for the doctor. After Dr. Carrel administered a local anesthetic, he probed the wound. Sherry could hear the grate of the hemostat on glass. The doctor pulled out little pieces of glass, one at a time. After about 15 minutes, he located the largest piece of glass and pulled it from deep within the wound. It was one inch long, brown, and shaped like a thin arrowhead. The patient asked to keep it to show his friends.

A little girl came in crying because she had a seed up her nose. It was plainly visible, and Sherry was able to extract it with a speculum and bayonet forceps.

The last case of the morning involved a teenage boy who complained of a fever. His temperature was 103°F (39.4° Celsius.) He was limping. A few questions, and the story came out. An abscess had developed on his left knee. After it drained, the boy felt better. However, he began having a painful lump in his left groin area and running a high temperature. Dr. Carrel prescribed an antibiotic injection and aspirin.

Sherry finished some of the never-ending paperwork, and made sure the doctor had seen all the lab results. Many patients had parasites, a result of drinking water from the river. The staff continually tries to educate people to drink only rainwater or boiled water.

Just after noon, Sherry went home for a fish and rice lunch. After a little rest, she was back to the hospital for the afternoon.

The afternoon shift was a little more calm because most patients were treated in the morning. One five-year-old girl had an abscess on her left elbow that needed to be drained, and an eight-year-old had fallen out of a tree. He had a painful, deformed forearm. Sherry set out the cast materials as the Brazilian nurse got the patient settled in. Within an hour, they had the abscess drained, the fracture reduced, and the arm casted.

As Sherry walked home from the hospital that evening, she was reminded that God was putting His character on display through the hospital team of which she was a part. She thought, *Nurses are definitely needed on the Amazon*. The irritations of the day were adding to the size of her pearl.

Some of the irritations come because people from North America have their own ways of doing things. Isn't that the right way? Shouldn't life on the Amazon be just like life in North America?

MYTH NO. 13

Life on the Amazon Is Like Life in North America

"Travel and communications are simple."

We all are captives of our own experiences, so we tend to assume that others live as we do. This is not the case, especially in developing countries, and even more emphatically in regard to travel and communications. Consider the following adventures.

Aviation Gas

When Tom Peace started flying in 1977, aviation gas was relatively cheap. In 1997, it was $6 a gallon—when you could get it. Keeping gas on hand, in the pipeline and paid for, is a constant challenge. Robbers can also reduce the supply of gas. The Benjamin Constant facility was robbed of several hundred dollars' worth of fuel.

In a January 1993 letter, ABWE pilot Clif Jensen wrote, "The fuel for the planes is almost gone, and there is still no response to our request to buy more. Permission must be given from the government each time we buy fuel. One barrel was for sale in Peru for a high price. Who knows? Maybe it is the gas stolen from us in May. If the man will come down to a price equal to what we normally pay in Brazil, I will buy it."

Sometimes the missionary pilots transport various government officials, and good can come from that. For example, in a hard rainstorm in 1983, Tom Peace set the plane down on the river to wait it out. When he started reading the Bible, Luco, his FUNAI passenger, started asking questions. After much discussion, Luco bowed his head to pray a simple prayer of faith in Jesus Christ. Was he genuine? Only the Lord knows. He appeared sincere. Since this agent speaks the language of the tribe he was servicing, something might prove useful in the future. No other Christian knows this language.

Flying Without Radio Contact

A loud clanging sound came from Tom's airplane engine at 5,000 feet on the last leg of his monthly evangelistic and supply flight. Tom had just finished listening to a cassette tape on the will of God, so he thought, *Lord, is this it? This situation must be Your will for me. You have to help me.* The clanging grew louder.

Checking the instruments gave no clue as to what was wrong. Tom thought there was smoke in the cockpit, but removing his sunglasses helped him see there wasn't. Throttling back, he directed the plane to the river. Landing, Tom pulled the plane up to a sandbar.

It was raining. Not wanting to spend the night in wet clothes, Tom climbed into the back of the plane to wait for morning or a let up in the rain. When the rain stopped, he got out, took off the cowling, and looked for the problem.

Oil was everywhere. Looking carefully revealed the problem: a cylinder had come loose from the engine block.

Tom found a settlement nearby where he engaged one man to guard the plane and another to take him back to Benjamin Constant in his motorized canoe. The man didn't want to start until the morning, so Tom stayed in the plane overnight.

Meanwhile, in Benjamin Constant, everyone was concerned. Beth Peace knew from radio contact with downriver missionaries that Tom had left them and should have been home by early afternoon. He wasn't. Newly arrived ABWE missionary pilot Mike Chiano and veteran pilot Terry Bower rushed to complete repairs on the mission's second plane so they could begin a search for Tom.

Just at dark, Terry quietly announced, "We'll go out looking again tomorrow." The Bowerses invited Beth to spend the night at their home. But Beth had learned over the years not to get upset even if Tom didn't return at the appointed time. She declined the Bowerses' hospitality. "I'll stay at home with our boys. Somewhere out on that river, he's okay."

The next morning, a motorized canoe appeared, but it was not the higher-powered canoe Tom had engaged. This one had only half the horsepower, which meant double the transit time. But it was the only transport available so, 13 hours later, Tom arrived back in Benjamin Constant. A ground-to-air radio in the plane would have saved a lot of emotional strain and time.

The Radio Tax

The government allows a pilot only 120 days from the time approval to get a radio is granted to the time the radio must be operable in the plane. Since missionaries must raise funds, that limited window constitutes a hardship.

Paying the radio tax proved to be a sanctifying experience for Tom. The right location to pay the radio tax was the bank, so Tom took his forms there.

- Mistake #1 was that three copies were required, but only two had been sent to the Peaces.
- Mistake #2 was the deadline date typed on the forms. The forms should have read *31-**03**-86*. Instead they said *31-**33**-86*.
- Mistake #3 was the out-of-date designation of Brazilian currency. Because of escalating inflation, the government had recently changed from *cruzeiros* to *cruzados*. The new *cruzado* was worth 1,000 of the old *cruzeiros*. In writing decimal num-

bers, the listing was automatically written in the old form of currency.

Because of the three mistakes, the bank would not accept payment for the radio taxes. Tom was told to go to the Federal Receipt Office in Tabatinga, 12 miles away by ferry. Arriving there he explained the three errors. The woman in charge typed out new copies. Three copies—error #1 solved. And the date was correctly typed 31-03-86—error #2 removed. But error #3 remained a problem.

Instead of rounding off the last number in the amount and moving the decimal, leaving the correct amount of 179.13 cruzados, she typed 179,134 cruzeiros. Tom explained that she should have left off the "4." The woman replied that, based on her past experience, she had typed the document correctly. Tom had to trust that her document would hold up elsewhere, or else he had to be disagreeable with her.

The following day was 31-03-86, so Tom took the papers in to pay the tax for the radio. The bank would not accept the forms because the Brazilian currency was still written incorrectly. Tom explained about the woman at the Federal Receipt Office. The teller went to the bank manager and showed him the problem. "No, we can't accept it." Tom pointed out the problem of not getting the matter resolved by that day's deadline date. The manager was sorry, but that was not his problem.

The manager suggested that Tom return a second time to the federal office and ask someone to retype three copies correctly, and ask them to extend the deadline one more day. Tom did. The woman at the federal office did her part. But time ran out, and Tom did not get back to the bank until the next day.

Arriving at the bank, Tom was told he was a day late, and they would not accept the forms. Bank authorities told Tom to go back to the Federal Receipt Office and ask the woman to type the papers over again and add two more days to the deadline. Tom did.

But a different woman was in charge of the office. Taking on a more authoritarian air than the previous worker, she announced, "No, we can't do this. You must send the papers back to Manaus."

"Thank you very much," Tom said as he hung his head and left the office for the two-hour ferry ride back to Benjamin Constant. Calling a missionary friend in Manaus, Tom explained the whole mix-up. A copy of the form was mailed to Manaus and taken to the State Radio Controlling agent. Eventually the problem was solved. Today, the mission plane has a ground-to-air radio.

School Vacation Homebound Travel

"How will we ever see our girls for Christmas?" Jack and Sandy Sorg asked each other. Each of their three daughters chose to finish high school in a mission boarding school with others their own age, instead of studying through home school or correspondence school. They didn't want to leave Mom and Dad, but they did want contact with others their own age. The Sorgs chose to enroll their girls in Fortaleza Academy, a school for missionary children almost 2,000 miles away, along the eastern coast of Brazil.

The school year created four opportunities for the Sorg family to be reunited. At the fall and spring breaks, the girls came partway home. They met their parents in Manaus, where Jack and Sandy went for periodic buying trips. At Christmas and summer breaks, the girls came all the way home to Santo Antônio do Içá via two planes and a boat. This trip home was tricky because the two plane trips had to synchronize with the boat, or the girls would spend many days waiting for the next plane and boat.

Coming home for Christmas one year turned into an adventure for 17-year-old Elizabeth and 13-year-old Suzanne. The first leg of the trip was by air. The airline was supposed to direct the girls safely onto the next plane for the second leg. Instead, they gave them their bags and literally shoved them out the airport door into the city of Manaus at midnight. Home was still 750 miles further west. Not knowing that any missionaries were in Manaus at the time, they phoned Judy and Eddy, a Brazilian couple, who borrowed money for a taxi and picked the girls up at the airport.

As this was unfolding, Dr. and Mrs. Sorg were waiting hundreds of miles away knowing nothing. Missionary colleague John Kallin was staying at the ABWE dormitory in Manaus. John found out that the girls were in Manaus and took charge of the situation. He rode with Elizabeth and Suzanne to the airport early the next morning to make sure they caught the plane.

Having traveled in Latin American countries, John and the girls knew they needed to get to the airport two hours before flight time, so they arrived at 8 a.m. for the 10 a.m. flight.

The usual long line was missing, but many disgruntled people milled around the huge lobby. The airline had decided to take off two hours early, and had already closed the check-in counter, located behind heavy, locked glass doors. John finally got the attention of one of the clerks, who opened the door a crack and listened to John's story about the bound-for-home girls. If the girls missed this flight, they wouldn't be home until after Christmas, and would have only a few days before they had to return to school.

By God's grace, the woman called the girls to come. Grabbing their suitcases, the attendants literally pulled them through the narrowly opened door—shutting out other passengers who tried to squeeze through. The door was instantly closed and locked. Elizabeth and Suzanne got the last two seats on the plane. Due to faulty phone service, Mom and Dad usually had no contact with their children from the time they left their school. All they could do was pray. God answered and that year the family had a merry Christmas.

Sandy Meets the Girls in Manaus

On one vacation, the girls flew from Fortaleza to Manaus. The parents' downriver boat trip to Manaus usually took a little under three days. Sleeping is a public activity, stringing up a hammock along with 150 other passengers.

Jack usually needed about ten days to complete his business in Manaus, so—depending on the medical needs at the hospital—Jack and Sandy would either arrive several days before the girls, or stay several days after the girls returned to school. On one occasion, Jack couldn't leave the hospital, so Sandy left about a week early with their son Matthew, to be able to greet the girls as they got off the plane.

Any of three ferries would get Sandy to Manaus in plenty of time. The first boat ended up on a sandbar before even reaching Santo Antônio, and would be out of service for days or weeks. The second boat tried to pull the first boat off the sandbar, and tore a small hole in its side below the water line!

By the time this second boat reached Santo Antônio, it was listing badly, and the captain warned new passengers not to embark. Jack forbade Sandy to get on. Even though the third boat was the slowest on the river, it was Sandy's only choice. When it passed Santo Antônio, Sandy and Matthew boarded and found hammock space. Each passenger selects his own sleeping spot on the deck from double-decker accommodations of hanging hammocks, although the passenger is responsible to provide his own hammock. With only three days remaining before the girls arrived in Manaus, Sandy hoped to be only four to six hours late. Jack called Brazilian friends Judy and Eddy. Would they please care for the girls again?

Still 500 miles from Manaus, Sandy's boat broke a propeller on a sand bar. Tugboats came from Manaus, pulling them off the sandbar and on to their Manaus destination. Extra days of travel meant the ferry ran out of food, water, and soft drinks. There was plenty of beer, however, and many of the passengers were becoming progressively more drunk. At 11 p.m. on the day before they were due to arrive in Manaus, Sandy and some other passengers prevailed on the boat captain to stop at a small city they were passing. They went door to door looking for a store owner who had water and food to sell. Finally satisfying Sandy and the few other sober passengers, the captain continued on to Manaus, pulled by two tugboats.

Sandy arrived in Manaus a day and a half after the girls. Neither those who had seen Sandy and Matthew off in Santo Antônio, nor those who expected them in Manaus knew what had happened. This low-water period normally averaged one ferry boat sinking per year. Travel and communications on the Amazon are not what they are in America. Missionaries are grateful for the prayers of God's people for provision and safekeeping.

Returning from Furlough

The plane and boat trips back to Santo Antônio do Içá were always an adventure, but especially after furlough, because the Sorgs had extra luggage. After one furlough they stopped in Manaus and purchased a new dog to help guard the house. The six-week-old Doberman could fit in a bird cage—the only travel container they had. The Sorgs arrived at the airport with luggage and dog two hours before flight time, but found their plane couldn't take off. A cargo plane had collapsed its landing gear and was blocking the runway.

The Sorgs were told to go home and wait for about 24 hours. After taking the dog out of his cage, and packing their luggage into a Volkswagen van, they went back to the mission apartment. Because savvy travelers don't leave the initiative with airport personnel, Jack decided to call back right away to make sure that airport workers knew how to reach them.

"Return immediately to the airport," Dr. Jack was told. "The plane is already loading." The Sorgs repacked everything and rushed to the airport.

But they weren't loading the airplane. They were loading buses to carry passengers to an old military air base on the other side of town, near the mission apartment—the exact direction from which the Sorgs had just come. The poor puppy had to be checked in at the bus, in his little bird cage, for the one-hour ride to the next airport.

The old military airport had no food concessions or water, except puddles on the floor from the last rain, and not enough chairs. Being experienced travelers, the Sorg family whipped out their peanut butter, jam, bread, and water, which they shared with two British ladies. They could hear their poor pup howling in the distance.

Because of the airplane delay, the Sorgs missed their ferry connection at the next stop. Freeing the puppy from its prison, they loaded their baggage into two speedboats during a light rain, and were off. An hour and a half later, they overtook the ferry boat at the next town. Boarding, they put up their wet hammocks. The poor dog still had not touched earth since early that morning and needed to! His initiation into the Sorg family didn't hurt the pup too much. Three months later, the Sorg Doberman could not fit his head into that cage.

Experiences of Santo Antônio Missionary Children

A jungle hospital allows missionary children to have experiences they wouldn't have in North America.

"Please let me see a delivery," pleaded Jennifer, the oldest Sorg daughter. This seemed a strange request since she didn't like to hear about blood, let alone see it!

Jennifer had been helping in the sterilization department during the summer school break as she mustered up the courage to observe a delivery. Only days remained before she would have to return to school.

Sandy waited until a patient arrived whom she thought would be an "easy" delivery. A mother who had five children at home, arrived in late labor with her sixth child. She hadn't had any prenatal care, so only after rushing into the delivery room with Jennifer, and setting up for the "quick and easy" delivery did Sandy discover the baby was a footling breech (coming out feet first). Sandy sent for Jack, who was seeing outpatients just around the corner.

As the baby's body was being delivered, Jack struggled to gently deliver the head. He then needed assistance with the lacerations and bleeding. The infant was not breathing, so Sandy needed help with the mouth-to-mouth resuscitation. Jennifer, who had always avoided the "grosser" parts of medicine, was now essential to both her mother and father as they worked to save both mother and baby.

Jennifer's doctor father talked her through opening materials for his sterile operative field, giving injections, and hanging IV's. Her mother talked her through opening resuscitation materials and sent her for the incubator and oxygen. With large eyes and a pale face, Jennifer faithfully helped until both mother and baby were doing well.

Sandy still hoped Jennifer would see a quick and easy delivery to balance off that experience, but Jennifer was content to finish out the summer in the sterilizing department.

Family Closeness, Even at a Distance

In 1988, Sandy and three-year-old Matthew returned to the United States for an operation on Matthew's ears. He was almost deaf from frequent ear infections. Dr. and Mrs. Bob Stough, of Roanoke, Virginia, kindly opened their home for the Sorgs to stay, arranged an appointment with a pediatric ear, nose, and throat specialist, and orchestrated the day for the surgery. Sandy and Matthew expected a precise and brief stay in the United States.

In the midst of that, Sandy became ill and needed a minor emergency procedure. The Stoughs graciously took care of both Sandy and Matthew.

At the same time, in Brazil, Suzanne, then 11 years old, told her father, "Daddy, my tummy hurts!" Looking at her pale, sweaty face, and palpating her tender right side, her dad realized Pepto Bismol was not going to cure this stomach ache; Suzanne had appendicitis. Jack faced the prospect of operating on his own daughter, something most doctors don't want to do.

The nearest surgeon and hospital Jack felt were capable of handling this type of surgery was 750 miles and three days' travel-time away. That was out of the question.

Young Suzanne was afraid of hospitals, injections, and especially surgery. She needed her mother to prepare her properly, but Sandy had just come out of surgery herself, hours before, in the United States. Jack had to find a different approach.

He arranged everything needed for the surgery: operating room, anesthesia, medicines. Then he carried the potent anesthesia ketamine home in a small syringe. Sitting on the couch where his daughter lay, he explained simply that he had some medicine which would take away her pain. Suzanne asked suspiciously if it was a pill or an injection. She knew she needed something, but her hopes clearly lay with a pill.

"An injection."

"When will I get it?" she asked. Since the anticipation of the injection was the worst part, he had given her the least time possible for her fears to multiply.

"Right now," he responded. Brandishing the injection, doctor dad moved swiftly but tenderly. In seconds, it was over. Over the next five minutes the medicine took effect, and Jack told Suzanne that when she woke up, she would feel better.

Once she was asleep, Jack picked her up and carried her down the dirt path 200 yards to the hospital. The staff and missionary personnel started an IV while Jack changed clothes for the operation. The appendectomy, thankfully, was uncomplicated.

Suzanne awoke that night in a hospital bed with her father beside her. He explained the surgery. An appendectomy is one of the few operations where the patient usually has less pain after the operation than before. Suzanne felt better, but had one request: she wanted to sleep in her own bed. So early the next morning,

Jack picked her up and carried her back home.

The next day was a special day which several ham operators had arranged the previous week. A three-way ham radio contact was made with Jennifer and Elizabeth at the Fortaleza Academy, Jack and Suzanne in the Amazon, and Sandy and Matthew in the United States.

That happy, long-distance reunion over the airwaves was broadcast to the whole world. The world heard the Sorgs' joy at finally talking to one another after weeks apart, the surprise as each one recounted unexpected surgery, and the assurances that everyone was doing well. Life on the Amazon is different from life in North America. We don't wait weeks without the possibility of communication as loved ones face surgery.

Everyone, no matter the location, has times of frustration, irritation, and disappointment. We may feel that the devil is working overtime to get us. Surely the devil wouldn't bother with the Amazon.

MYTH NO. 14

The Devil Is Too Busy to Bother with the Amazon

"What is the Cross Movement?"

The evil one is actively opposing spiritual progress. Much is stacked against the advancement of truth. The cancerous spirit of the universe is ready to stir up trouble, division, and misunderstanding to further his nefarious evil.

First, having held title to the people of the Amazon for millennia, Satan is not too busy to defend his turf. Many people still live in unvarnished animism and spiritism, knowing nothing of the living God or His Son, Jesus Christ our Redeemer.

Second, Satan is ready to distort whatever spiritual light is available. For example, when a woman was desperately ill, she resisted going to the Amazonas Baptist Hospital. Why? Because she was sure that the kindness and love shown was treachery. She believed patients were turned into canned meat and shipped to North America as dog food. Or think of the local witchdoctor. When he sees death coming, he tries to get the sick person to the hospital in time for the Christians to be blamed for the patient's demise.

Satan uses many tactics to maintain his stronghold on the Amazon.

The Cross Movement

This group began in 1977 when, returning from his fields, Irmão José found his wife in bed with another man. Enraged, he found an ax and used it.

It is believed that Irmão José was raised by a fervent Pentecostal mother and a nominal Roman Catholic father. Having respect for the Bible, he combined hatred of images with a cram-it-down-your-throat zeal.

A few days after the axing incident, when Irmão José had cooled down a bit, he felt tremendous conviction about what he had done, and feared he would never go to heaven.

Thinking he had killed both his adulterous wife and her companion, Irmão José fled to Peru where he lived for several years.

At confession, the Roman Catholic priest told Irmão José to do an act of penance. From his background, Irmão José believed he had to do a mighty work for God to have any hope of obtaining salvation. So Irmão José willingly vowed to become a slave to Jesus Christ and plant one thousand crosses all over the region to atone for the supposed murders. The people of the Cross Movement always display a 20- to 30-foot-high painted wooden cross in the middle of their villages. Veteran Brazilian missionary John Kallin said, "I was told by a Cross Movement follower that Jesus lives inside the cross. If you cut the cross, it will bleed. Jesus can see everything going on around it. Within one hundred yards of the cross, all is holy, so people must not smoke, drink, or sin in this area." When asked who Christ was, Cross Movement followers say He was the One who sanctified their cross for them. Carved into the cross are the letters STA, initials from Portuguese words meaning *save your soul*.

Several years and several hundred crosses later, after a TV interview, Irmão José learned that his wife was still alive.

The Act of Penance Turns Into a Religious Group

From the start, this group was a protest against the sins Roman Catholics winked at. At his direction, Irmão José's followers wore long sleeves, long skirts, and sought to show minimum skin despite 100°F weather. He called his religion the True Catholic Church, or the Apostolic Catholic Church, saying the Roman Catholic Church was apostate because it allowed idols. The Catholic bishop was enraged, but Irmão José held his ground.

In the beginning, most followers were non-Indian, educated people, and comparatively wealthy. Gradually they were expelled from the Irmão José movement for various sins, leaving the rank and file of the movement to the poorer, less educated Indians.

Irmão José settled in the town of Jui on the Içá River, and leaders from Cross Movement settlements came to him for training in leadership and doctrine. Leadership conferences occurred every several months, with people coming and going all the time. John Kallin said, "When we were in Jutaí, the Cross People would return from their training to teach 'the latest' at the local level. At prescribed times, they would walk through town in a procession, dressed in white, carrying a large cross, and singing songs from the Baptist and Pentecostal hymnbooks. Each congregation was well organized with a president, vice president, and apostles as leaders."

Eventually, the movement came into conflict with the Roman Catholic Church. Irmão José became so radical that the Roman Catholic Church cut him off, contrary to their general policy of inclusiveness. Eventually, Irmão José became sufficiently radical that the government started opposing him. His followers armed themselves with knives and guns to resist federal control of their stronghold, Jui, the center in all of the Amazon for this cult.

With some 3,000 followers holed up in Jui, no police, federal authorities, or missionaries could get in. In this Jim Jones-like cult, loyal Indians and some Brazilians were enslaved to their would-be messiah. Disobedience from the "faith" required hours of kneeling before the cross to show proper penance.

John Kallin reports his encounter with the Cross Movement as follows:

"After holding meetings with Ticuna Indians in the area, we were able to start a church in the town of Feijoal. When Irmão José came through, however, we were put out of the area.

"One of the Cross Movement men attacked me. In God's grace, his baseball-style swing (instead of hitting from the top straight down) struck only a glancing blow.

"When the Brazilian Army got involved, along with the Ticuna church, and suggested that we go elsewhere for awhile, we did. A Ticuna believer, however, moved to Feijoal, started a school, and continued the gospel witness.

"By asking questions, I pieced together a profile of this movement. The largest landowner of the area converted to and became a leader in the Cross Movement. But his motives were suspect; a bigger village meant more customers for his store. His sins soon distanced him from the movement's guiding principles. Cross Movement people moved onto his property in Feijoal, soon outnumbering the Baptist believers. The Baptists were told, 'Convert or move out.' They did not want to leave the land they had cleared, or the village they had founded.

"When we resumed meetings in Feijoal, the Cross Movement people didn't like it. They threatened, 'If you come here, soon everyone will be Baptist. God's judgment is coming on you. Read about that in the book of Revelation. Escape this coming judgment by erecting a cross. Towns with crosses and 100% Cross Movement worshipers will escape. All other places will fall into the river and perish—including Feijoal, if it has part Cross Movement followers and part Baptists."

Though he promised the faithful he would return from the dead to lead them, eventually Irmão José died and stayed dead.

A second leader arose from the ranks in Jui, a long-bearded man, even more radical, but less powerful and popular than Irmão José.

In April 1996, a bank manager named Aldeney, who is a member of the church in Benjamin Constant, was visited by a person from the Jui Cross Movement. Unable to deliver truth about God, the Jui man reported that the movement was getting weaker. "The people are searching for God. Will you visit us?" he asked.

Aldeney, Pastor Josué, a missionary pastor from south Brazil, and ABWE missionary pilot Al Yoder jumped in the airplane and flew to Jui with fear and trepidation. Al reports, "We circled the area a few times thoroughly, then set her down."

Not trusting the airplane to the people, Al stayed with it. He invested the waiting time sharing the gospel with people gathered around. He also asked them about their beliefs to gain a better understanding of their situation.

As the pilot witnessed to the people, the pastor and the bank manager took the one-mile canoe trip to the main village. The meeting at Jui was tense. In the dark, incense-laden meeting place, the pastor and Mr. Aldeney expected to meet the head man of the movement. Instead, they met another leader who sat with a Bible in one hand, and a gun within arm's reach.

The pastor spoke, "We are not here to interfere; we are not here to fight you. We have come to help you. We can offer you the services of the airplane when we are here. We can bring in medical supplies, but we mostly want to offer you Bible training if you will allow that."

The gun-toting man replied, "No one comes here without our permission. Others have tried to come. They preach and yell and scream in the streets, and we escort them out. But we like your approach. You are welcome in our town."

Fifteen minutes after the meeting began, the trio were homebound with a canoe-load of fruit and an invitation to return!

Three more visits followed in the next few weeks. The evangelistic team hesitated to do anything without the blessing of the captain (village leader), who was absent. Lest it look overly aggressive, presumptive, or even hostile, the team resisted their desire to hold meetings and teach the Bible.

Even though the captain still had not returned by late July 1996, around 300 people came to the edge of the river to hear Mr. Aldeney and Al Yoder speak. The men gave an explanation of the gospel, then said, "We can't hold a proper service because your leader is not here. We want him to be present. We want to respect your territory."

As the men tried to leave, the airplane started backfiring. Al had left most of his tools behind in order to reduce the weight of the plane as much as possible and allow it to land on a small patch of water by the main Jui village. Damage to the engine increased by the second as it continued to backfire; take-off looked as far away as the moon.

Shutting the plane down, Al uncovered the engine. Adding insult to injury, he lost his glasses and a needed tool that fell into the water. Al recalls praying, *Lord, this is not fair. You have given us a miraculous opening to these people, and now it all seems to be hanging in jeopardy. I'm working for You, Lord. What will happen to this plane if I have to leave it here? And how will we get home?* By airplane, the trip takes only 40 minutes, but a low-powered speedboat trip would take 40 hours.

"I was trying to trust the Lord, and He was trying to teach me once again, as He has many times: 'I'm in control,'" Al admitted.

With the cowling off, nothing looked wrong. The pilot racked his mental diagnostic files. Everything testable with limited tools proved all right. Timing in the magneto? Reaching into the hot engine, Al burned his hand and arm, raising immediate blisters.

"Lord, what are You trying to teach me?" Al cried. He says, "God wanted to teach me that I was trying to get out of there too fast."

Just then, the man from Jui who had invited the evangelistic team to come in the first place, paddled up to the plane and said, "I want to tell you a secret. The main leader is getting weak. He doesn't want to lead anymore. We are trying to elect a new spiritual leader as of next week. The new man is the one who likes you guys. So pray hard. You may be able to take over the church here."

Now they knew why God had delayed their departure: to bring great encouragement to them and to enlist their prayer. Al prayed, "Lord, now we know why You allowed us to delay. Now help me see what's wrong and how to fix it."

The moment he opened his eyes, Al saw a tube on the intake at the back of the engine that had come loose. Why he hadn't seen it before? A Swiss pocket knife, some innovation, and 15 minutes later they flew out, carrying the encouraging news.

The missionaries were excited. If the people in the town of Jui come to Christ, doors to preach the gospel in over 1,000 Cross Movement churches and villages will open.

The devil is not too busy to bother with the Amazon, but God is more than his equal. Sometimes God works in miraculous ways.

THE STORY OF ABWE'S MEDICAL WORK

ON THE AMAZON

JUNGLE MYTHS

Brian and Karen Williams in riverboat hammocks.

Above:
Jack Sorg, checking a patient at the ward.

Left:
The Amazon River.

Cristóvão hospital evangelist, preaching on hospital verandah.

Amazonas Baptist Hospital

Lab worker and hospital evangelist, Cristóvão.

Above:
Hammocks, the bed of choice for many Brazilians.

Left:
A woman from Santo Antônio.

A macaw

Above:
Side view of Amazonas Baptist Hospital.

Left:
Sleeping quarters on a riverboat.

Amazon Indians at Bible Institute.

Typical river "taxi."

A Ticuna song leader.

Boy on a makeshift boat.

CWE team members who helped with construction of the hospital addition. (*Front row, far left:* Dr. Mark Thompson, with his wife Donna immediately behind; *Front row, far right:* Dr. Jack Sorg.)

MYTH NO. 15

Baptists Don't Believe in the Miraculous

Or do they?

Wednesday morning, March 24, 1997, dawned clear in Boa Vista, Roraima, the northernmost international airport in Brazil. This leg of the trip, to St. Vincent in the Caribbean, was given a good weather bill of health.

Church-planting pilot Al Yoder and Matt Cropsey, adult son of ABWE missionaries to Togo Dr. Robert and Shirley Cropsey, had left Benjamin Constant, Brazil (at the junction of Peru, Colombia, and western Brazil), flown downriver to Tefe, then angled north/northeast to Boa Vista on the second day's flight. So far, the two days had been uneventful, though the light craft had bucked foul weather most of the way.

The plane, in service on the upper Amazon since 1966, was being flown back to America for a thorough overhaul. Hank Scheltema, Director of ABWE's Aviation Ministry and Al's father-in-law, had originally flown the aircraft to Brazil and registered it 30 years before. Only 100 hours of flight time earlier, Al, a certified mechanic and inspector, had replaced all the engine's cylinders. So while engine problems were far from Al and Matt's minds, weather wasn't.

At 7:30 a.m. EST, Al and Matt buckled themselves into the cockpit, lifted off, and flew north toward the mountains separating the Amazon Basin from the Caribbean and the coast of Guyana. Pleasant flight.

Coaxing the plane up to 12,500 feet to cross the mountains was difficult. Scanning the dials for overheating, Al found nothing to worry about. Uneasy because of the plane's resistance at climbing to less than ideal altitude, Al turned and headed for a lower pass through the mountains, where he could safely cross to an alternate landing location already listed on his flight plan. This was a logical response since maps aren't precise for this area of the world, in spite of modern satellite mapping methods. Most elevations are listed as "estimated."

Back in the United States, two men stood by as flight-following contacts: Hank Scheltema in Georgia, himself a veteran of Amazon Basin missionary aviation, and Bill Sill in Pennsylvania. The plane's short-wave radio—rather than the normal airplane radio—gave Al and Matt significantly greater communication capacity. Hourly contact with Hank and Bill apprised them of their status and the terrain over which they flew.

At 8:30 a.m., Al made contact, reporting the change in destination. The weather worsened; clouds closed in so that the world below was a grayish-white soup. Only the mountain peaks poked through, looking like spikes nailed through a sheet of plywood. But visibility was good and turbulence minimal at 9,500 feet. Matt was napping.

About 9:15, it happened: a loud explosion in the engine! Cockpit peace was instantly shattered; urgency driving the eyes and brains of both men as they sought the reason.

Al remembers being angry that his wife, Kim, was going to become a widow. Feeling silly that his mind had raced ahead to that extreme conclusion, he refocused his energies on the crisis at hand. The engine continued running, but with less power, and it vibrated badly.

"Mayday! Mayday!"

Bill responded immediately from his home; Hank minutes later from Atlanta. The invisible 1,800-mile umbilical cord would soon be carrying death-defying information to the pilots.

The Lord Is My Shepherd, I Shall Not Want

Fighting to stretch out the plane's glide path, Al estimated the plane was losing altitude at the rate of 400 feet per minute. Al and Matt did their best to plot a course between the mountain peaks as they descended into the soup; "estimated" mountain elevations didn't help. The whole situation had turned grim. Up north in the States, Hank and Bill frantically gathered charts and maps, looking for landmarks Al and Matt might be able to use.

The little plane sank into dense clouds, and was lashed by rain. Waiting somewhere below was the hard ground, cushioned by trees 300 feet tall. From the air, the jungle looks like unending miles of giant broccoli: soft, nourishing, even inviting. But once below that deceptive vegetation, few come back—the last seven planes to take that plunge hadn't. The mountain peaks on either side waited silently to envelop the tiny plane.

From Atlanta, using information provided by the global positioning system (GPS), Hank was able to steer Al toward a local river. Since the plane could land on both runways and water, a river normally meant a safe landing spot.

The Amazon River at many places is miles wide and drops only 400 feet in 3,000 miles (Hank calls it the longest runway in the world). The Cuyuni River—where Hank was directing Al and Matt—drops 450 feet in only 100 miles and boasts 75 whitewater rapids. Yet it held their best hope for a safe landing.

He Leadeth Me Beside the Still Waters

At this point, Al and Matt had been flying blind for 35 minutes. How close were they to a mountain? Were the 300-foot trees about to snare them? Minute by minute, the drama continued. That radio voice—a whole continent away—proved comforting.

Assured by Hank that the GPS coordinates showed a place to

land, Al and Matt flew on. Breaking through the clouds at 1,500 feet, they were encouraged to see they were well above the trees, but no river was in sight. Nearby, they saw threatening mountain peaks thrusting up into the clouds. Al steered toward Georgetown, Guyana's capital, hoping to get as close to the city as possible.

Flying over a ridge, they suddenly saw the river! The plane was doing better in the heavier atmosphere and lower altitude, and holding steadier in the rich air. Al turned to follow the river, hoping to reach the coast and Georgetown.

It wasn't to be. The plane stopped holding altitude. Knowing they must land, Al looked for the best stretch of river and plotted his approach. Circling, they passed over a barge—civilization! People!

Most landings are made against the wind to slow the aircraft, but the situation here was the opposite. Not good, but at least the water was smooth, not whitewater rapids. The length and narrowness of the river would be tough—too short and too little room to maneuver.

"Loosen your seat belt, Matt. We may have to get out fast," Al told his co-pilot.

Once committed to the landing, Al had cut off the airplane's power, so they came down hard. Hard enough to force one float completely under the water. Before they could move to get out, the float popped above the surf. The tailwind turned the powerless airplane toward the riverbank, and directly ahead loomed a large tree. Planes normally slow quickly against the drag of the water on the floats. But that wasn't happening this time.

"Brace for impact!" yelled the captain.

In the providence of God, the tree was rotten and disintegrated like a feather pillow. The cushioning tree absorbed the crash energy and barely scratched the plane. They were down, safe and unhurt. Even the airplane, engine troubles aside, was in good shape.

Leaping out onto the floats, Matt and Al grabbed shoreline vegetation to anchor the plane against the strong current. They tied up the plane.

He Restoreth My Soul

Back on the radio, Al shared the good news of their safe landing with Hank and Bill. Conserving battery power was now a major factor. They agreed to less frequent and shorter transmissions.

The current still had the potential to damage the airplane. As Al and Matt worked to ensure the plane's safety, they heard an engine in the distance. Around the bend came a motorized canoe from the barge they had flown over. These men were gold miners operating a suction barge.

The area was known to be on the drug traffic route north, and small planes are the transportation of choice in that trade. The miners were suspicious, but were eager to help and won over by the deportment and composure of the two missionary pilots. They contributed food, water, and communications assistance. Al and Matt advised the Guyanese authorities that they had landed safely, but needed assistance. They waited with their aircraft.

Thou Preparest a Table Before Me

Assured that the two men were down safely, Hank switched hats. The radio navigator turned diplomat. Hank Scheltema had become experienced with South American governments during his 20-plus years as a missionary pilot. He had served many Peruvians, Colombians, and Brazilians with emergency medical flights. Humanitarian service rounded out his knowledge of these and other nations. Brazil had given Hank its Peacemaker Medal.

Hank called the office of the president of Guyana, then fired off the following fax to that office:

URGENT URGENT URGENT URGENT

AIRCRAFT CESSNA PT-CJG (AMPHIBIAN) FORCED DOWN BY ENGINE FAILURE ON CUYUNI RIVER WEDNESDAY, MARCH 12 AT 9:45 A.M. ATLANTA, GEORGIA TIME. COORDINATES: 6 DEGREES, 47 MIN-

UTES, 87 NORTH, 59 DEGREES, 58 MINUTES, 86 WEST. PILOT ALLEN YODER, CO-CAPTAIN MATT CROPSEY ARE USA CITIZENS. I HAVE BEEN IN CONTACT BY AMATEUR RADIO. PLEASE SEND HELP AT ONCE AS THEY ARE IN DANGER. THANK YOU FOR YOUR KIND HELP.

HANK SCHELTEMA, DIRECTOR OF INTERNATIONAL AVIATON FOR THE ASSOCIATION OF BAPTISTS FOR WORLD EVANGELISM.

But Guyana was not indebted to Hank. So even this veteran experienced difficulty reaching the authorities in Guyana. Calling their embassy in Washington, D.C., he learned the reason. President Cheddi Jagan had died, and the nation's attention and resources were focused on his funeral.

Hank contacted Air Search & Rescue in Miami and Puerto Rico for any assistance they could give. The Miami office aided their communication with the Guyanese officials. But four hours passed before Hank heard from a Guyanese deputy. Provided with more information, the deputy promised to send a helicopter out, but not until the next morning. That discouraging news came first, then Al's radio battery went dead. Now, on site, face-to-face communication was the only way to help. Hank had to get there!

He Leadeth Me in Paths of Righteousness

At the river, Al and Matt opened the cowling to inspect the engine. Before the radio died, they had been able to tell Hank that a cylinder had blown, and the explosion had knocked off the exhaust system on the right side of the engine. The piston head had blown apart from the barrel, making visible a one-inch gap.

From years of servicing airplanes, Hank created a list of possibly needed parts and hunted for them. Hank was pleased to discover that a recent parts shipment from the supplier included a few more things than he had noticed when he inspected the shipment previously—including the essential cylinder.

The next morning, a Guyanese Army Air Force helicopter flew over the downed Cessna. It brought the federal police and the leader of the Civil Air Patrol to inspect the plane. They were touchy about paperwork and leery of drug traffic. Small airplanes arouse suspicion. Even though Hank had quickly arranged visas for Al and Matt by phone, officials started hassling the downed fliers.

The officials inspected the damaged airplane engine themselves. Colonel Michael Charles, the helicopter pilot, feeling an *espirit de corps* toward fellow pilots and knowing they had been through a grueling situation, stepped in to shield the two men from further examination. Colonel Charles was amazed that they had landed safely.

Al and Matt were airlifted to a nearby airstrip and then boarded a flight to Georgetown.

Another pilot, Colonel Miles Williams, was also a protector. "We know what you are going through—forced down in a strange country." Williams stayed with Al and Matt through six hours of interrogation and debriefing by the civil police, federal police, and Customs and Immigration officers. Finally at 8 p.m. on Thursday, the paperwork was in order, and the two weary travelers were officially welcomed to Guyana.

Meanwhile, back in the States, Hank scrambled to arrange a flight south, get the parts he had ordered sent directly to Miami, make arrangements to meet Bob Cropsey, Matt's dad, and get on to Georgetown. With everything he could think of and find on short notice, he was en route to Miami by 11 a.m. The rendezvous in Miami was smooth, but the flight to Georgetown was canceled. The only other flight was overbooked, due to the earlier cancellation.

By explaining the emergency situation, Hank and Bob were able to get seats. Arriving at Timehri International Airport at 1 a.m. Friday, they were warmly welcomed by Al and Matt. By 2:30 they were in bed.

In the Presence of My Enemies

Time was an enemy. The clouds and rain, through which Al and Matt had descended, were having their normal effect: rising water. The miners reported that the river was rising fast. More water meant stronger currents which would endanger the aircraft.

Up at 7:30 a.m., Al and Hank scavenged for parts Hank hadn't known he needed to bring with him. The U.S. Ambassador, Ms. Heibern, was helpful in making contacts which produced a needed exhaust system from Guyana Sugar Corporation.

With everything in hand, Al called the Army Air Force to see about getting a chopper lift back to the river. Colonel Charles was busy and could not take them until the next day, unless they could be ready to leave in one hour. They were.

Arriving at a sandbar one mile from the plane, the pilots asked the miners to help them ferry the plane to the sandbar, where it would be easier to work on the engine.

The miners had been pumping out the floats, protecting the plane against the current and doing everything they could to keep the plane safe.

It was 6 p.m. on Friday before work on the engine could begin. Exhausted from accumulated stress, the men worked until 10 and then decided to get some sleep.

But the water was still rising. At the rate it was rising, their makeshift sandbar repair outpost would be under water in fourteen hours. So by 2:30 a.m. they were back at work, using flashlights in calf-deep water, with little fish nibbling at their legs. A can of oil tipped over on the tools, making them slippery and hard to grip. Occasional thunder was answered by howler monkeys from trees on both sides of the river.

By 11 a.m., they had reassembled the engine and done the test runs. Al did a solo test flight, not wanting to risk any additional weight until the engine was proven and he'd had a chance to navigate a tricky take-off from the winding river.

The chopper, due back to take the men out, was delayed. With the river rising, and their sandbar all but gone, the men decided to fly out in the repaired Cessna. Take-off required the plane to gain speed around a bend in the river and leap into the sky before the trees claimed them. With full power on the newly repaired cylinder, Al coaxed the plane up to airspeed, and lifted her over the trees. Although not as difficult as the landing, take-off proved a tense moment. They landed PT-CJG at Timehri International at 1 p.m. to a hero's welcome.

My Cup Runneth Over

At 7:30 Sunday morning, Al Yoder and Matt Cropsey lifted into a brilliant sky. Trinidad, Antigua, Puerto Rico, Turks & Caicos, and Miami on Monday. Their original flight plan showed a Miami arrival on Thursday, so they were four days behind. But consider their excuse: They had lost an engine cylinder over mostly unmanned mountains, descended through more than one mile of clouds among peaks, found and crash-landed on a rocky, twisting river in the one open stretch for miles, landed as suspects and left in the good graces of the government, met helpful miners, worked through the bureaucracy of Guyana, got the necessary parts, repaired the engine, flew the plane out and in good shape, and made new friends in the process, leaving as heroes.

I Will Fear No Evil (Psalm 23)

While most Baptists believe that miracles are not the normal way God works today as He did in New Testament times, we do believe that He is doing things which clearly show His supernatural intervention. God is not restricted to what man thinks He should do. God will fulfill His purpose anywhere in the world.

Epilogue

Onward!

When ABWE organized the Central Amazon region field council, medical care was scarce. Missionaries expecting additions to their families went to Iquitos, Peru, or returned to North America. Later on, the government established clinics and hospitals in a few areas, but had trouble keeping good doctors.

Missionaries living 100 or more miles downriver had to rely on their own knowledge of medicine, usually learned from hands-on experience, and from the trusty *Merck Manual*. Missionaries such as Lindsey and Jean Harrell recall those early days. Jean says, "One time a Brazilian man came to our house with his hand dripping with blood. He had slipped in his canoe. His shotgun fired, leaving a gaping wound between his thumb and forefinger. Another time an eight-year-old boy climbed up to where the fishing gear was stored. When he fell, a six-inch-long fishing hook caught him in the upper abdomen. Then there was the man who managed to get a spear lodged in the outside edge of his right knee joint. We cleaned people up and treated them as best we could. We treated malaria, worms, and other illnesses, and wished for a hospital. A hospital might have been able to help the woman who fell out of a tree onto a sharp bush stump, causing internal bleeding. We wished we had a hospital close enough to take the 15-year-old girl who bled to death delivering twins."

The Harrells were still in Brazil when construction of the Amazonas Baptist Hospital began in 1983.

God's Change of Plans

Jack and Sandy Sorg were the ABWE missionaries whom God used to initiate the hospital ministry. They had dedicated their lives to the Lord and planned to spend a lifetime serving along the Amazon River. Because of multiple allergies to molds and grasses, doctors told Sandy, before she ever went to the Amazon jungle, that was not where she should serve as a missionary. Feeling God had called her along with her husband, Sandy headed to Brazil with her young family. To the Sorgs' pleasant surprise, she actually improved at first.

After ten years in Brazil, the allergy symptoms increased, but were still controlled with over-the-counter medicine. On furlough, the Sorgs lived in an air-conditioned house which decreased the mold and pollens in the southern United States climate.

Returning to Brazil in 1992, the Sorgs weren't prepared for the severity of Sandy's allergic reaction. Climbing off the plane in Tabatinga, they gathered up their luggage for the boat ride. The boat had already left. A heavy rainstorm started, preventing them from renting a speedboat to catch up with the ferry in the next town.

Sitting in a small cafe at the water's edge, they met the owner and operator of the ferry, who was finishing business in Tabatinga. He planned to catch up to the ferry in a large, comfortable speedboat after the storm subsided, and offered the Sorgs a ride. Grateful for the opportunity, they waited. Hours later, the storm slackened to a heavy, cold mist and the owner's fast watercraft departed, racing to catch the ferry before nightfall.

Arriving so late, the boat was full. Every hammock space was taken. The Sorgs had to be content with a small space along the rear corridor, just outside the busy toilets. They strung their hammocks over one another in the narrow space. Through the night, the dust, mold, and diesel fumes wreaked havoc on Sandy.

Over the next several years, Jack increased his wife's medicines but she gained only marginal improvement. Sandy became limited to working for a short time in the air-conditioned surgical area of the hospital, or in her air-conditioned bedroom. Asthma and sleepless nights continued to sap her strength.

During the same period, the only other doctor in the area left. Jack was now the only physician for an area with a population of 50,000 people. The hospital's spiritual ministry was booming, with professions of faith occurring week after week. Boatloads of patients arrived from sections of the river that had no previous contact with the gospel. In those glorious early months of 1995, more people heard the gospel for the first time than at any time since the hospital doors were opened.

But Jack became exhausted with the continuous night calls. Sandy went to the hospital for deliveries several nights a week so Jack could sleep. Then the Sorgs found that their young son Matthew's dyslexia was worse than they had thought. Sandy's home schooling, which she had done successfully for the three girls, was not working with Matthew. By mid 1995, Sandy was able to be out of bed only four or five hours per day. Due to shortness of breath, she couldn't walk the 1,000 feet to church.

Back in the United States in 1995, Sandy had extensive tests which confirmed the Sorgs' conclusion: allergic asthma, with special sensitivity to molds, dust, and pollen. Treatment for a year and a half didn't help. When Jack brought home a dusty, moldy book from the Amazon, her asthma reacted to the book.

By mid-1997, hopes of returning to the hospital full time were extinguished. Sandy's physicians warned she would not live more than a few months in that climate.

Over the two years in the States, Jack and Sandy visited their supporting churches, and Jack commuted to Brazil every two to three months for preaching, medical work, and hospital documentation work.

The very day Jack told the ABWE administration they could not return as missionaries to Brazil, Dr. Robert Cropsey told ABWE that his family—who had been on an extended medical leave in the USA—would be able to return to Togo. Dr. Cropsey had been the International Director of Medical Missionary Enlistment for ABWE. Jack was offered the position. God's timing is marvelous.

God Is Raising Up a New Team

Dr. Chip and Laurie Phillips: Gordon R. Phillips III (Chip) and Laurie Delp Phillips were accepted as ABWE missionaries to Brazil in 1994. Chip and Laurie had been married while Chip was a surgical resident at the State University of New York in Buffalo.

Saved at the age of seven, Chip dedicated his life to the Lord at age 13. During his medical training, he went on a short-term trip to Haiti. Following Laurie's nurses' training, she served short term at the Amazonas Baptist Hospital. As a couple the Phillipses went to the ABWE hospital in Togo for short-term service, and when they joined ABWE full time they were headed for Africa. However, God changed their direction, and when Chip completed his trauma fellowship at the University of Philadelphia, and earned his M.S. in Bible from Philadelphia College of the Bible, the family headed to Amazonas, Brazil.

Chip, Laurie, Reed, Caleb, and Allison arrived in Manaus, Brazil, on November 20, 1996. Three days later Chip traveled to Santo Antônio do Içá for field council meetings. During his brief visit Chip toured the hospital, met the national and missionary staff, and familiarized himself with the town.

Language study began with the new year in 1997. Because they had already started training while still in the United States, the Phillipses had a headstart. Chip assisted a seminary student with outreach at 12 daughter chapels, providing accompaniment and special music on his guitar. In addition to witnessing and other contacts during language study, Chip and Laurie focused on obtaining the necessary Brazilian licenses to practice medicine. Laurie rotated at a dermatology hospital, while Chip assisted in the operating room at one facility and joined student rotations at the state's tropical disease referral center.

In May of 1997, Chip spent 10 days in Santo Antônio do Içá, seeing 135 patients with complaints ranging from snakebite, to cataracts, skin diseases, and malaria. Later that year, he spent an additional two weeks at the hospital, translating and coordinating construction work teams from the U.S. which were expanding the hospital facilities. On September 14, 1997, Chip's paperwork was formally submitted for Brazilian medical licensure.

While Chip and Laurie's personal license paperwork was in process, progress was being made on obtaining official recognition of the Amazonas Baptist Hospital as a non-profit facility. The success of that petition would drastically reduce the government's imposed taxes from 40% to 15%. Chip worked with various officials to speed up the approval process, which moved as slowly through the legal system as did the Phillipses' personal applications.

February 1998 marked the dedication of the newly enlarged Amazonas Baptist Hospital. When Chip and Laurie moved their family to Santo Antônio, Chip assumed all hospital administrative responsibilities, as well as general maintenance duties. Because his formal government license to practice medicine was still pending, Chip was limited to performing only emergency procedures such as appendectomies and C-sections. Chip also helped with music at the Faith Baptist Church in Santo Antônio, and started Bible studies with two men in town. One Bible study was with a 16-year-old whom Chip had led to the Lord and began discipling following an emergency appendectomy at Amazonas Baptist Hospital. Chip and Laurie met regularly with one of the church leaders for accountability and encouragement.

In addition to this doctor-and-nurse team, the Lord has called Dr. Mark Thompson and his wife, Donna (another nurse), pharmacist David Buckalew, and his wife Teri, and nurse Carolee Graf. Others are committing themselves to the work at the Amazonas Baptist Hospital.

Without a doubt, the new team at the Amazonas Baptist Hospital will face bureaucratic hassles, natural disasters, and the attacks of Satan. They will experience sickness and health, joy and sorrow, trouble and triumph. But God will be with them through it all, and HE IS NOT A MYTH.

Who's Who in ABWE on the Amazon

(Listed by year of arrival)

1944 *FLODEN, Orville & Helen*

The pioneer missionaries who organized the work in Leticia lived on a boat in their first years, ministering up and down the river. They adopted Elizabeth, a Colombian child. Their home in Leticia was an open door to all missionaries who came for mail, medical care, or relaxation. Orville initiated the ham radio operation called *BRAG (Baptist Radio Amateur Group) NET*. One of Helen's favorite expressions was: "It's the decisions that get ya!" A fellow missionary said of Orville, "He died an unsung hero." Along with many other missionaries, the Flodens are spoken of by Brazilians with deep affection and great respect. Both are now with the Lord. They served with ABWE from June 1943 to May 1975.

1946 *ROGERS, Blakely & Mary*

Blake served as a pharmacist's mate in the Coast Guard during WWII. During his overseas duty in the Caribbean, he became impressed with the need for missionary work in Latin America. While he was a student at Philadelphia School of the Bible, the couple began attending the ABWE weekly prayer meetings. The very day after hearing a letter from the Flodens asking for a couple to come to help them, the Rogerses volunteered. They were known for their evangelistic zeal, and early issues of the *Message* magazine tell of people they won to Christ. In the 1960's the Rogerses became houseparents at the Oak Crest Missionary Children's Home. They later returned to serve in coastal Peru until retirement in 1972. They now live in Florida.

1950 LOONEY, *Jack & Joyce*

Besides the medical work they both were involved in, Joyce started a Christian day school. They also worked with a church in Benjamin Constant and, in the 30-foot boat Jack built, did river evangelism on the Jauari, Itui, and Itacoari rivers. The Looneys resigned from ABWE in 1967.

1951 SCHLENER, *John & Fran*

This couple worked the Amazon River with his brother and sister-in-law, Paul and Jessie, from The Port of Two Brothers. The Schlener brothers made an enormous impact on the lives of the Ticuna Indians and helped establish 12 churches. In 1973 John and Fran moved to southern Brazil where they served at the São Paulo Baptist Seminary. Later, John was the ABWE Representative for northwestern U.S. They retired in November 1981 and now live in Spokane, Washington.

1951 SCHLENER, *Paul & Jessie*

These Schleners served God for almost 40 years on the river; and helped establish 12 churches that went on to be pastored by Indians, including large churches in Tabatinga and Campo Alegre. "Paul was dentist, mechanic, school teacher, and comedian," said one missionary. "He always had great one-liners and kept us laughing. A wise man." Paul and Jessie served with ABWE from October 1950 until February 1991. They live in Moses Lake, Washington.

1953 *HARRELL, Lindsay Edward & Jean*

The Harrells first arrived in Benjamin Constant, where they organized and established a church. Moving to Santo Antônio do Içá, they sought to establish a multi-cultural church. When it was not possible to mix the two cultures, Lindsay and Jean became the champions and architects of Betânia, the Ticuna Indian village of about 2,000 people 15 miles from Santo Antônio. Using the Portuguese version of his middle name, local people called him Eduardo. Older people still talk of the kindness shown to them by Eduardo and Jean. The Harrells lived, loved, and served among the Ticunas from 1953 to 1987. Now retired, they live in North Carolina.

1957 *POULSON, Ralph & Marge*

When they first arrived in Brazil, the Poulsons served a term in Benjamin Constant as a pastor and Christian school teacher. In the early 1960's they moved to Natal, Brazil, to teach in the ABWE school. They served with ABWE from 1956 to 1981 and now pastor a church in Ferndale, Washington.

1958 *PAYNE, Dale & Martha*

These pioneer missionaries in Santo Antônio do Içá were the first ABWE missionaries to work with the Ticuna Indians. Martha was an excellent children's worker and VBS director. Both worked at camp and also did medical and dental work. In 1973, they transferred to south Brazil, where Martha served in the Regular Baptist Press in São Paulo. Even after their retirement in 1996, they returned to Brazil to help revive a dying church. The Paynes served in various parts of Brazil from 1956 to 1996. They now live in Englewood, Colorado.

1960 BLAKSLEE, *Edward & Dorothy*

The Blakeslees initiated a medical ministry and established a church in Fonte Boa, 300 miles east of Santo Antônio. They continued the medical and evangelistic work, and developed congregations along the Atti-Parana River. Edward served as mission business coordinator in Manaus. They served with ABWE from October 1958 until June 1983, and now are involved in missionary work in El Paso, Texas.

1960 SCHELTEMA, *Hank & Ruth*

Hank ferried an Aeronca Sedan on floats and set up operations at Benjamin Constant in 1960. That marked the beginning of ABWE's aviation ministry which included starting new preaching points in previously difficult-to-reach places, delivering supplies to missionaries in remote places, and providing emergency air lifts. Hank often had to give medical care, including once removing a gangrenous hand. Perhaps that is why in December 1977, Hank presented to the Field Council an 11-page report called "The Prospective Medical Missionary Ministry for Amazonas." Hank took the Sorgs on a survey trip; this book details the outcome of that trip. The Scheltemas returned to the U.S. in 1979 and assumed the position of Southern Representative for ABWE until he was needed back in the Central Amazon. In 1993 Hank was made the ABWE International Administrator of Aviation. In this position he locates aircraft for missionary service, oversees aviation work in the countries where ABWE operates this work, recruits, and works with pilots joining ABWE. Hank routinely closes his correspondence with the words "Up in the air for Him."

1963 BOWERS, *Terry & Wilma*

Terry was the second ABWE pilot on the Amazon River. He flew to speak at several preaching points and was much loved by the people in the interior. In 1982 Terry became the administrator for the language school in Manaus. After working in Tabatinga for one year, health problems took the Bowerses home to Michigan; and Terry on to Heaven on July 6, 1991. Wilma lives in Michigan; a son and his wife, Jim & Roni Bowers, are ABWE missionaries in Iquitos, Peru.

1967 *WANTOCH, Lois*

Lois was the first ABWE single woman missionary to arrive on the upper Amazon. Her life and example opened the door for other singles to follow. Lois served in Santo Antônio do Içá until 1975, doing medical and midwifery work that was foundational for the hospital. She served in Foz do Jutaí from 1976–1988, and from 1989 to the present in Tabatinga. This native Nebraskan, who runs on coffee, is an excellent teacher and discipler—and even a dentist, when needed.

1968 *WRIGHT, Robert & Rita*

Appointed with ABWE in 1966 after spending 10 years in Brazil with another mission, the Wrights moved directly to St. Rita in 1968 while the Scheltemas were on furlough. They built a house in Campo Alegre and worked directly with the Ticuna Indians, part of the missionary team that taught the Ticunas about evangelism and church growth. Since 1977, Dr. Wright has served as missions professor at Western Baptist College in Salem, Oregon. Since 1984 he has been involved in Romania, where he helped establish a Bible Institute under national leadership and continues to provide resources.

1968 *KALLIN, John & Sylvia*

Following language school in 1968, the Kallins served in St. Rita, Campo Alegre, Betânia, and Benjamin Constant from 1969–1974. From 1975–1998 they worked as church planters in Foz do Jutaí. Currently they are serving at the hospital. These steady soldiers of the cross call the Minneapolis/St. Paul area home when they are in North America.

1976 PEACE, *Tom & Beth*

Born in Mule Shoe, Texas, Tom was called to missions later in life. Tom is a fine preacher and a friend to the local people. Required to fix everything with nothing, Tom is an able mechanic —a valued skill when resupply is 750 miles away in Manaus. Tom was a church-planting pilot based in Benjamin Constant from 1977–1990; since 1990 the Peaces have been based at the hospital in Santo Antônio do Içá. Beth helps in obstetrics and general nursing, assists in the pharmacy as necessary, and cares for the hundreds of guests in their home. Iowa is their base when they are in the U.S.

1978 SPOELHOF, *Bill & Sue*

Appointed to the Amazon in 1977, they were delayed by visa problems. They finally received government permission to live in São Paulo, where they completed language training. Bill and Sue were able to move to the Amazon in 1982; Bill taught at the MK school in Manaus for one year before the Spoelhofs went on furlough. From 1984–1986 Bill taught MK's in Santo Antônio. Some of the challenges he faced included one child in each grade from kindergarten through eighth grade; chasing snakes and chickens out of the school building; and enduring the interested spectatorship of local townspeople. In addition to teaching missionary children, Bill started a choir in the local church and directed several cantatas. The Spoelhofs helped in the church's building projects, directed Sunday school, and Sue trained children's workers. When the field council asked them to help with the hospital administration in Manaus, the Spoelhofs moved once again and remained from 1986–1988. At that time, they relocated back to São Paulo, where Bill continues teaching in the seminary to this day.

1980 *SORG, Jack & Sandy*

Jack was the chief medical officer of the Amazonas Baptist Hospital from its opening in 1985 to 1997. Jack was also the prime mover in the construction of the original hospital building, and enlisted Paul Puleo's *Construction for Worldwide Evangelism* out of Tampa, Florida, to build Phase II, an expansion that doubled the square footage in 1997–98. Sandy was a nurse, midwife, and anesthesiologist at the hospital until health needs and children's education needs forced them to leave the Amazon. She now watches over the homefront as Jack travels in his new assignment as International Director of Medical Missionary Enlistment.

Of the Sorg family, Thomas Finch of the Stone Mountain Baptist Church in Georgia wrote, "Handyman to surgeon; carpenter to counselor; father and friend; preacher and teacher. Sandy: nurse and mother; homemaker and friend; animal keeper (she picks up strays—the two-legged kind and the four-legged kind); compassionate and concerned about 'how my patients are doing; must make one final call to the hospital before bed.'"

1980 *YODER, Al & Kim*

The Yoders' first assignment was in Bahia, Brazil, although Kim was no stranger to the country. Her parents are Hank and Ruth Scheltema, and Kim grew up in Brazil. In February 1989, the Yoders transferred to the church-planting aviation ministry then based in Benjamin Constant. Al's duties included medivac flights to the hospital, as well as ferrying guests in and out. Al has helped organize preaching points in places such as Sururua, Novo Progresso, Belém, and São Paulo de Olivência. He served in two Bible institutes, one in Benjamin Constant for Brazilians, and one in the Port of Two Brothers (Santa Rita) for Ticuna Indians. Al also launched COMAS, an organization in the Benjamin Constant–Tabatinga–Leticia area to assist in fulfilling the Great Commission. The majority of leadership and membership of COMAS is Brazilian.

1981 *HAWLEY, Dr. Bill & Patricia*

Along with Jack Sorg, Bill Hawley is remembered as one of the founders of the Amazonas Baptist Hospital. Bill was a gifted Bible teacher who was fluent in Portuguese. He enjoyed ministering to people both medically and spiritually. Patty loved the Brazilians and enjoyed entertaining them in their home. The Hawleys worked at the hospital until family health problems required them to return to the U.S. in 1990. They were active in their local church and returned as short-term missionaries to the hospital from time to time. In 1997 Bill was diagnosed with inoperable cancer, and on August 13, 1998, went to be with the Lord he served so well.

1981 *SHARP, Carolynn*

This Canadian came to the Amazon as a nurse and assisted Jack Sorg in establishing the hospital. Carolynn's colleagues call her "dedicated," "a good organizer," and "great on follow-up and making sure things are done right." Carolynn is responsible for training national nurses; supervising sterilizing in the Central Supply Department. She also gives valuable, faithful service in the operating room. Carolynn continues to serve at the Amazonas Baptist hospital.

1981 *BAKER, Mark & Debby*

The Bakers served as church planters and in seminary administration in Manaus from 1981–1991. Mark was also instrumental in hospital construction, buying, and finance, all of which involved mountains of paperwork. They now live in Davenport, Iowa.

1981 *JENSEN, Clif & Hannah*

The Jensens arrived to serve on the Amazon as pilot, church planter, teachers, and trouble-shooters for the church in Benjamin Constant. During their stay in that city, they formed a friendship with Jaco Gomes and eventually led him to the Lord. After studying at the Bible Institute in Benjamin and seminary in Natal, Jaco Gomes became the pastor of Faith Baptist Church in Santo Antônio do Içá. The Jensens returned to the U.S. in 1992 and now are involved in a camp ministry in Tennessee.

1981 *THOMSON, Sue*

After serving as a summer intern in Peru, Sue completed courses in X-ray tech, attended Moody Bible Institute, and came to work in the Amazonas Baptist Hospital. In addition to the X-ray department, her duties included hospital payroll manager and bookkeeper, and hospital buyer. She also taught part time at Faith Bible Institute and worked with young people at Faith Baptist Church in Santo Antônio. Sue worked with Mary Ann Thompson to direct the young people in presenting a superb play from the book of Daniel. She spoke Portuguese fluently and was loved by the Brazilians and her colleagues. Sue served until 1994, when she returned to the United States to care for her elderly parents.

1982 *CHIANO, Mike & Teresa*

Teresa had been a single missionary working with Lois Wantoch in women's and children's ministries. She met Mike when he came to Brazil on a Missionary Apprenticeship Program. Mike served as a pilot on the Amazonas field from January 1987–1990. Health factors forced them to withdraw after three years of service. They now live in New York.

1986 *THOMPSON (ZWYGHUIZEN), Mary Ann*

Before going to the Amazon, Mary Ann served with her sister Christine in Togo, West Africa, for seven years. Although nursing was her major responsibility at the Amazonas Baptist Hospital, she also was the hospital pharmacist and helped in administration by doing inventory, purchasing, record keeping, and personnel management. "Ask Mary Ann," was an often-heard remark. Mary Ann had a good ministry in the local church and as the director of discipleship at the hospital. She will long be remembered for writing a drama about the fiery furnace story in the book of Daniel. During the young people's enthusiastic performance, the church caught on fire! Mary Ann served in Santo Antônio do Içá until 1994. She is now Mrs. Zwyghuizen and lives in Grand Rapids, Michigan. But Thompsons continue to serve at the hospital; her brother Mark and his family arrived in 1999.

1987 *SKIRROW, Sherry*

This registered nurse from Brantford, Ontario, Canada, first went to the Amazon in 1981 on a Missionary Apprentice Program. Returning for full-time service, Sherry runs the outpatient department, fills prescriptions, supervises the cleaning staff, assists in surgery, and—on occasion—in anesthesia. Concerning working in the operating room, she echoes others who describe that department as "Hours of boredom, moments of terror." Sherry was acting director of the hospital during a year when no doctor was available. She also teaches Sunday school and one-on-one Bible studies, and mentors nationals.

1995 *WILLIAMS, Brian & Karen*

The Williamses initially served out of Benjamin Constant, filling in for the Yoders, who were on furlough. While constructing their own home during their first term, they also met many needs in hospital maintenance and food service. Karen taught Sunday school, and every evening they welcomed young people to play volleyball at their home, building contacts and relationships that could develop into spiritual opportunities. Their role is church planting, leadership training, river evangelism, and hospital assistance.

1997 *KOCH, Emmett & Terron*

The Kochs arrived on the field with their four children, Glen II, Ellen, Luke, and Alice, to begin language study in late 1997. The Kochs will make good use of their training as educators as they move into their church-planting work.

1997 *PHILLIPS, Dr. Gordon (Chip) & Laurie*

The Phillipses took cross-cultural experience with them to the Amazon. Chip had been on a short-term missions trip to Haiti. Laurie had served short term as a nurse at the Amazonas Baptist Hospital; and together they had worked at the ABWE hospital in Togo. During language study in 1997, Chip was the translator, logistical coordinator, and back-up medical officer for one of the construction teams that expanded the hospital in 1997. In February 1998 they moved to Santo Antônio where they have also been involved in Bible studies and music ministry at Faith Baptist Church. Susanna Leigh was born at the Amazonas Baptist Hospital on November 1, 1998, joining Gordon IV, Caleb, and Allison. The saga of Dr. Phillips trying to obtain his medical license in Brazil will be the basis for the next book!

1998 *DULL, Shelah*

The summer after graduating from college, Shelah went to Amazonas, Brazil, on a missionary apprenticeship program. While there, she was invited by the missionaries to return that same year to teach MK's, which she did for two years. Shelah was appointed full time to Brazil in 1996, and arrived in 1998 to begin language study. When her language training is complete, Shelah again will teach missionary children and assist the local church.

1998 *GRAF, Carolee*

After receiving her nursing degree Carolee spent two months in the spring of 1997 working at the Amazonas Baptist Hospital. That summer, she attended ABWE's candidate class and was appointed to Brazil. Carolee arrived in the country in 1998 to begin language study. When that is complete, she anticipates working at the Amazonas Baptist Hospital.

1999 BUCKALEW, *David & Teri*

During a missions trip to Argentina with their church, God spoke to the Buckalews concerning full-time service for Him. When they learned the Amazonas Baptist Hospital needed a full-time pharmacist, they felt this was the place God had chosen for their service. Throughout the book we have read of nurses and doctors running the pharmacy out of necessity. David will be able to run this important department more efficiently, and together the Buckalews will evangelize and disciple local people.

1999 THOMPSON, *Dr. Mark & Donna*

The brother of Mary Ann Thompson, Mark served two short-term stints in Santo Antônio. In a beautiful jungle romance, he courted and later married Donna Wuthrich, who was serving at the hospital as a nurse at that time. The Thompsons were in the 1996 ABWE candidate class and returned to the Amazonas Baptist Hospital as career missionaries in February 1999.